Y0-AEW-382

Monticello

Mon

Th. Jefferson
MONTICELLO
CHARLOTTESVILLE, VA.

NATIONAL
GEOGRAPHIC
WASHINGTON, D.C.

ticello

THE OFFICIAL GUIDE TO
Thomas Jefferson's World

Contents

A TIMELINE OF
JEFFERSON'S LIFE, PAGE 13

"THE WORDS OF THOMAS JEFFERSON"
EXHIBITION IN THE SMITH GALLERY, PAGE 33

THE UNIVERSITY
OF VIRGINIA,
PAGE 128

Introduction

Leslie Greene Bowman

PRESIDENT, THOMAS JEFFERSON FOUNDATION

PHILOSOPHER, REVOLUTIONARY, president, connoisseur, gardener, epicure, diplomat, scientist, educator, innovator, and farmer, Thomas Jefferson was, *is*, the essential architect of American life. The most complex and fascinating of the Founders, he is a man of the seemingly distant past whose contradictions and achievements speak to our own time. Relentlessly interested in the hopes of humanity, he gave us the epic words of the Declaration of Independence, and he brought both substance and style to the new nation. His home and masterpiece, Monticello, is a touchstone for all who seek to explore the enduring meaning of "Life, Liberty and the pursuit of Happiness."

We are proud to bring you this guide to Jefferson's beloved home, and to share with you the stories of this extraordinary place and its designer.

On a little mountain in Charlottesville the power of place merges with the power of Jefferson's timeless ideas. Monticello was the center of Jefferson's world; to understand him, you must experience Monticello, his autobiographical statement. Monticello comprises a house, an ornamental landscape, a farm, and a revolutionary garden, including orchards and vineyards where Jefferson experimented with more than 300 varieties of fruits and vegetables.

Monticello was also a working plantation—where the paradox of slavery stands in stark relief to the ideals of liberty expressed by Jefferson in the declaration. As a result of Jefferson's assiduous record keeping, and more than 50 years of scholarly research by curators, historians, and archaeologists, Monticello is among the best documented, best preserved, and best studied plantations in North America. Our work illuminates the lives of those enslaved at Monticello—their families, work, skills, hopes, and dreams.

EACH YEAR MORE than 430,000 visitors travel to Jefferson's mountain, and millions more experience Monticello through our website and digital platforms. When you visit, you will discover a world-class museum—the only American home on the United Nations World Heritage List and a national historic landmark—and a center of scholarship and historical research.

French President François Hollande with Leslie Greene Bowman and
President Barack Obama in Jefferson's Cabinet at Monticello.

The Thomas Jefferson Foundation was incorporated in 1923 to
"preserve Monticello as a memorial to Thomas Jefferson and his ideas."
Monticello survives and inspires today because the Foundation, which owns
and operates Monticello, has been dedicated to its dual mission of preservation and education for over 90 years. The Foundation has painstakingly
worked to restore Monticello, seek out original furnishings, reacquire
plantation lands, and expand educational programs—engaging millions
of people in a dialogue with Jefferson and his ideas.

AS A PRIVATE, NONPROFIT organization, the Thomas Jefferson
Foundation receives no regular federal, state, or local governmental support.
We rely on the private support of our donors to empower our capacity to
preserve and educate. Donors to the Foundation are stewards not only
of Monticello, the three-dimensional autobiography of Thomas Jefferson,
but also of Jefferson's enduring ideals—of personal liberty, religious choice,
and the illimitable freedom of the human mind.

Thomas Jefferson

When Rembrandt Peale painted
this portrait in 1805, Jefferson
was the nation's third president.

A MAP of
the moſt INHABITED part of
VIRGINIA
containing the whole PROVINCE of
MARYLAND
with Part of
PENSILVANIA, NEW JERSEY and NORTH CAROLINA
Drawn by
Joshua Fry & Peter Jefferson
in 1751.

To the Right Honourable George Dunk Earl of Halifax First Lord Commi
and to the Rest of the Right Honourable and Honourable Commiſsioners for TRADE and PLAN
This Map is most humbly Inscribed to their Lordships,
By their Lordships
most Obedient & most devoted humble Serv.ᵗ Tho.ˢ Jeffer

A Man of the Enlightenment

ON APRIL 13, 1743, THOMAS JEFFERSON was born into a world of privilege and responsibility. His father, Peter Jefferson, was a successful tobacco planter and surveyor. His mother, Jane Randolph, belonged to one of Virginia's most prominent families. Thomas was 14 when his father died in 1757, leaving Jane to raise six children and run the plantation at Shadwell, Virginia.

At age 17 Jefferson enrolled at the College of William and Mary in Williamsburg, Virginia. Six feet two and a half inches tall, with reddish sandy hair, he was brilliant and precocious, moving easily in the capital's sophisticated circles. Under Professor William Small, Jefferson studied the works of Isaac Newton, Francis Bacon, and John Locke, whose Enlightenment thinking rejected established authority in favor of reason, knowledge, and natural rights. After graduation, he practiced law and served in the House of Burgesses, where he heard orators like Patrick Henry speak. At 21 Jefferson inherited a landed estate and began building his home at Monticello—a project that occupied his imagination throughout his life.

No man has greater confidence, than I have, in the spirit of our people." —Thomas Jefferson

14
JEFFERSON'S AGE
when his father died

33
JEFFERSON'S AGE
when he wrote the Declaration of Independence

On New Year's Day, 1772, Jefferson married Martha Wayles Skelton, a 23-year-old widow who shared his passions for literature and music. During a decade together, they had six children, only two of whom survived to adulthood. When Martha died in 1782, Jefferson was devastated, burying her in the family cemetery at Monticello. He never remarried.

Along with land surrounding Monticello, Jefferson also inherited slaves from his father and father-in-law. Although he recognized slavery as a "moral and political depravity," Jefferson owned slaves his entire life. In a typical year at Monticello, he owned about 130 men, women, and children, almost half under the age of 16. Several enslaved families lived at Monticello for more than three generations, including the well-known Hemings family. Most scholars believe that, years after the death of his wife, Jefferson was the father of six children with Sally Hemings.

LIFE-SIZE BRONZE SCULPTURE OF JEFFERSON BY IVAN SCHWARTZ WITH STUDIOEIS, 2009

BELL USED BY MARTHA
JEFFERSON TO SUMMON
ENSLAVED SERVANTS

Martha Wayles Skelton Jefferson

Called Patty in her youth by family and friends, Martha Wayles Skelton Jefferson was born in 1748 on the plantation of her father, John Wayles, about 25 miles northwest of Williamsburg, Virginia. She was a widow when she married Jefferson in 1772, having lost both her husband, Bathurst Skelton, and three-year-old son, John. Described as possessing "considerable powers of conversation, some skill in music, all the habits of good society," she was also said to have "a vivacity of temper which might sometimes border on tartness." She died on September 6, 1782, four months after giving birth to Lucy Elizabeth, her sixth child with Jefferson. As one granddaughter remarked, "her loss was the bitterest grief my grandfather ever knew."

DETAIL FROM A PAGE IN MARTHA
JEFFERSON'S HOUSEHOLD ACCOUNT BOOK

Hostilities between Great Britain and the American colonies had begun in 1775, when Jefferson was elected as a delegate from Virginia to the Second Continental Congress in Philadelphia. Impressed by the eloquence of his previous writings, the Congress asked Jefferson in 1776 to draft the Declaration of Independence, in which he proclaimed that all men have equal rights, regardless of birth, wealth, or status, and that the government is the servant, not the master, of the people—ideas that have inspired generations around the world.

Following two terms as Virginia's governor, Jefferson was appointed in 1784 by Congress to take a post in Paris, first as a trade minister and then as minister to France. During this period, he deepened his fondness for European culture, later bringing home to Monticello books, seeds and plants, works of art, furniture, and scientific instruments.

In 1790 he joined Washington's Cabinet as secretary of state, an appointment marked by his opposition to the pro-British policies of Alexander Hamilton, who was secretary of the treasury. Six years later, Jefferson lost his first bid for the presidency to John Adams, falling short by three electoral votes. He served instead as vice president. Four years later, he defeated Adams to become the nation's third president. Jefferson's most notable achievements in office were the launching of the Lewis and Clark expedition to explore the American West and the purchase of the Louisiana Territory in 1803, which doubled the territory of the United States.

Nothing made Jefferson happier than leaving Washington in 1809 to return to Monticello. Ten years later, in nearby Charlottesville, he laid the foundation for the University of Virginia. He was 83 when he died on July 4, 1826—the 50th anniversary of the Declaration of Independence.

81

JEFFERSON'S AGE
when the University of
Virginia opened

MINIATURE OF JEFFERSON IN
1788 BY JOHN TRUMBULL

« THE TIMES

Jefferson Time Line

1743 Born at Shadwell on April 13.

1757 Father Peter Jefferson died.

1760 Attended the College of William and Mary.

1768 Elected to House of Burgesses in Williamsburg. Began construction at Monticello.

1770 Shadwell burned. Moved to South Pavilion outchamber at Monticello.

1772 Married Martha Wayles Skelton. Daughter Martha born.

1775 Elected to Continental Congress. Daughter Jane Randolph died.

1776 Drafted Declaration of Independence. Elected to Virginia House of Delegates. Appointed to revise Virginia laws. Mother Jane Randolph Jefferson died.

1777 Drafted Virginia Statute for Religious Freedom, passed by General Assembly in 1786. Unnamed son born and died.

1778 Daughter Mary (Maria) born. Brickwork of Monticello I completed.

1779 Served as governor of Virginia until 1781.

1780 Began *Notes on the State of Virginia*.

1781 British troops at Monticello.

1782 Daughter Lucy Elizabeth born. Wife Martha died.

1784 In France as a trade minister and minister to France until 1789. Daughter Lucy Elizabeth died.

1790 Served as first secretary of state.

1797 Served as vice president until 1801.

1801 Served as president of the United States until 1809.

1803 Louisiana Purchase concluded. Lewis and Clark expedition launched.

1804 Daughter Maria Jefferson Eppes died.

1809 Retired to Monticello.

1825 University of Virginia opened.

1826 Died at Monticello, July 4.

Declaration of Independence

A Revolutionary Philosophy

PENNED AT A MOMENT OF CRISIS, Jefferson's bold declaration "that all men are created equal" not only put forth the argument for the creation of a new nation, but also made a claim for universal rights. As Abraham Lincoln later wrote, Jefferson's enduring and visionary words "gave hope to all future mankind." ❁

DRAFTING THE TEXT

Entrusted by fellow delegates with preparing a Declaration of Independence from Great Britain, Jefferson retreated to his Philadelphia boardinghouse on June 11, 1776, to draft a "common-sense" account of their actions. The mahogany lap desk (right) on which he wrote the declaration was of his own design, built by Philadelphia cabinetmaker Benjamin Randolph, with whom Jefferson lodged when he first came to the city. Not long before he died, Jefferson gave the desk to his granddaughter Ellen Wayles Randolph Coolidge and her husband. Today it's owned by the National Museum of American History in Washington, D.C.

86

CHANGES

were made to Jefferson's draft by the Second Continental Congress.

FELLOW PATRIOTS

Despite their many differences, Jefferson's revolutionary generation (below) was bound together by a commitment to establish a new nation based on radically different ideas. The Declaration of Independence, Jefferson wrote, was an "expression of the American mind."

GEORGE WASHINGTON   JAMES MADISON   THOMAS PAINE   JOHN ADAMS

"... our attachment to no nation on earth should supplant our attachment to liberty." —Thomas Jefferson

Declaration by the Representatives of the UNITED STATES AMERICA, in General Congress assembled.

When in the course of human events it becomes necessary for one people to the political bands which have connected them with another, and to among the powers of the earth the separate and equal station to the laws of nature & of nature's god entitle them, a decent respect opinions of mankind requires that they should declare the causes impel them to the separation.

We hold these truths to be self-evident; that all men are created equal, that they are endowed by their creator with inherent & inalienable rights; that among these are life, liberty, & the pursuit of happiness; that to secure these rights, governments are instituted among men, deriving their just powers from consent of the governed; that whenever any form of government becomes destructive of these ends, it is the right of the people to alter abolish it, & to institute new government, laying it's foundation on principles & organising it's powers in such form, as to them shall most likely to effect their safety & happiness. prudence indeed dictate that governments long established should not be changed for & transient causes: and accordingly all experience hath shewn that kind are more disposed to suffer while evils are sufferable, than to themselves by abolishing the forms to which they are accustomed. but a long train of abuses & usurpations [begun at a distinguished period, pursuing invariably the same object, evinces a design to reduce under absolute Despotism, it is their right, it is their duty, to throw off such & to provide new guards for their future security. such has the patient sufferance of these colonies; & such is now the necessity constrains them to expunge their former systems of government. history of the present King of Great Britain is a history of unremitting injuries and usurpations, among which appears no solitary fact to contra—

JEFFERSON SUBMITTED HIS "ROUGH DRAUGHT" ON JUNE 28. AFTER FOUR DAYS OF DEBATE, A REVISED VERSION WAS ADOPTED ON JULY 4.

Little Mountain

PETER JEFFERSON LEFT a sizeable estate to his son, including the mountain where Thomas would build his "essay in Architecture." In an entry to his Garden Book on August 3, 1767, the name Monticello appears for the first time. Jefferson didn't leave definitive evidence why he chose the name, but he was familiar with Italian and considered *The Four Books of Architecture* by 16th-century Italian architect Andrea Palladio to be his architectural "bible." In that book, Palladio says the ideal setting for a country house is atop a "hillock," or *monticello* in Italian. In addition, the Albemarle County Deed Books listed the name Little Mountain, so perhaps Jefferson simply translated the existing name into Italian (as he did with neighboring High Mountain, naming it Montalto).

✳ THE HOUSE

Architectural Influences from the Ancient World

MAISON CARRÉE AT NÎMES, FRANCE

STATE CAPITOL BUILDING IN RICHMOND, VIRGINIA

The impact of Jefferson's work on American architecture was recognized in 1993 when he was posthumously awarded the American Institute of Architects Gold Medal for "a significant body of work of lasting influence on the theory and practice of architecture." To find Jefferson's influences, one must turn to designs from the ancient world. One such monument is the Roman temple at Nîmes, France, which he chose as his model for the design of the Virginia State Capitol. During his years in France, Jefferson's interest in antiquity deepened. He commented, "from Lyons to Nismes I have been nourished with the remains of Roman grandeur." Andrea Palladio's *The Four Books of Architecture* illustrated ancient buildings as well as his own villas, and perhaps had the strongest influence on Jefferson's designs; references to Palladio are found throughout Monticello.

EGLISE SAINTE GENEVIEVE, PARIS, COMPLETED 1780; NOW KNOWN AS THE PANTHEON

> *Mr. Jefferson is the first American who has consulted the fine arts to know how he should shelter himself from the weather."*
>
> —Marquis de Chastellux

MARQUIS DE CHASTELLUX

A major general in the French expeditionary force, François Jean de Beauvoir, the Marquis de Chastellux, helped the Americans defeat the British at the 1781 Battle of Yorktown. Upon returning to France, he wrote *Travels in North America,* his memoirs of early America including his 1782 visit to Monticello.

1767

THE YEAR

Jefferson first used the name Monticello in an entry into his Garden Book

ROLLING HILLS

From an early age, Jefferson had a view of the mountain that would become his home, seen below in "Monticello and Montalto from Edgehill," by Russell Smith. Its 867-foot peak stood just across the Rivanna River from his father's plantation, Shadwell, where he was born. The Shadwell Mill can be seen at center-left on the right bank of the river. Long before the first stone of his house was placed, he enjoyed many hours there reading with childhood friend Dabney Carr.

Neoclassical Architecture
Jefferson's System

THOMAS JEFFERSON PIONEERED a new style of architecture in America. Emulating what he called "the beautiful monuments" of the ancient world, he helped to introduce the young nation to the neoclassical movement. His approach to architecture was largely influenced by Andrea Palladio. In his 1775 plans for Monticello's exterior, Jefferson used two of Palladio's interpretations of architectural orders,

ANDREA PALLADIO

No source shaped Jefferson's architecture more than *The Four Books of Architecture* by the Renaissance architect Andrea Palladio, one of the most influential architects of all time. From Palladio's publication, Jefferson learned about ancient Roman buildings, including the architectural orders, as well as Palladio's own designs from villas in the Italian Veneto. Born in Padua, Italy, in 1508, Palladio was first a stonecutter who eventually became the chief architect of the Republic of Venice. His style, called "Palladian," has been admired and copied throughout Europe and in America from the colonial era to modern times.

5
EDITIONS
of Palladio's *Four Books of Architecture* were owned by Jefferson.

"architecture is my delight, and putting up, and pulling down, one of my favourite amusements." —Thomas Jefferson, as recalled by Margaret Bayard Smith

Doric for the first floor and Ionic for the second. Jefferson's architectural knowledge expanded fully during his years in France, where he marveled at the Hôtel de Salm in Paris and the Maison Carrée at Nîmes. Monticello and the University of Virginia earned UNESCO World Heritage site recognition in 1987 for Jefferson's "significant contribution to neo-classicism." ✸

5

ARCHITECTURAL ORDERS
were illustrated by Palladio: Tuscan, Doric, Ionic, Corinthian, and Composite.

DOME ADVOCATE

Domes are perhaps the best known feature of Jefferson's architecture, as seen in his 1819 drawing for the south elevation of the Rotunda at the University of Virginia. His passion for the shape began while visiting the great domed market Halle au Blé in Paris, which, as he learned, was based on the ideas of 16th-century architect Philibert Delorme. He applied Delorme's method at Monticello and the Rotunda. The same principles were used to construct the first dome of the United States Capitol Building in Washington, D.C.

VILLA CORNARO
Built in the 1550s near Venice, Italy, this Palladio-designed home is a classic Renaissance villa. Its two-story column-faced facade inspired Jefferson's design of Monticello I.

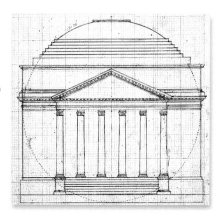

Monticello I

JEFFERSON'S INITIAL PLAN for Monticello had just 8 rooms, much smaller than the 21-room house he later built. On the first floor was a large parlor, flanked by a dining room and a chamber. On the second floor were a spacious study and two bedrooms. As a self-taught architect, Jefferson chose a neoclassical design that was stylistically ambitious and constantly evolving. Around 1775 he added a room to each side and a canted bay projection to the southwest front. Though not built for Monticello I, as this version is called, plans were developed during the 1770s for dependencies hidden in the hillside and linked to the house. It was this version that Chastellux remarked "resembled none of the others seen in this country."

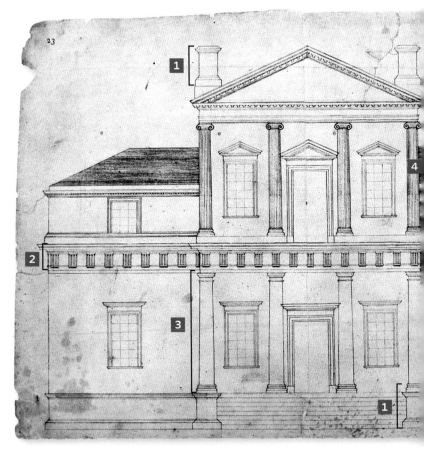

This first known drawing of Monticello, by Jefferson,
shows the west elevation of Monticello I before
the octagonal bows were added around 1775.

" *The Underpinning of the house should be at least one fourth of the height of the first story.*" —Thomas Jefferson

ANTIQUE STYLE

The design of Monticello I adhered strictly to classical rules of proportion. According to contemporary reports, the interior was also to be decorated in the style of Roman antiquity, though it is unlikely that plastering or moldings were finished by the time that Jefferson departed for France.

1784

THE YEAR

Jefferson halted construction of Monticello to begin his diplomatic mission in France

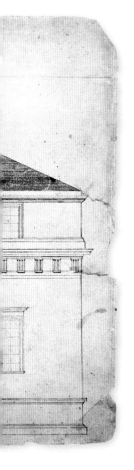

1 FOLLOWING PALLADIO, JEFFERSON CHOSE DORIC PEDESTALS FOR THE LOWER PORTICO, WITH MATCHING CHIMNEYS.

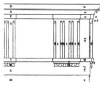

2 FOR THE FIRST STORY, JEFFERSON SPECIFIED AN ENTABLATURE OF THE DORIC ORDER AROUND THE PERIMETER OF THE HOUSE.

3 THE COLUMNS ON THE LOWER PORTICO WERE OF THE DORIC ORDER.

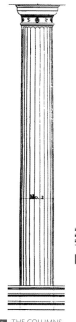

4 FOR THE UPPER PORTICO JEFFERSON SELECTED IONIC COLUMNS, WHICH HAVE VOLUTES, OR SCROLLS, ON THE CAPITALS, OR TOPS.

Thomas Jefferson in France

A Kindred Spirit

"**Y**OU ARE PERHAPS CURIOUS TO KNOW how this new scene has struck a savage of the mountains of America," Jefferson wrote to a friend from Paris. He'd been sent there as a trade negotiator in 1784, and the following year he succeeded Benjamin Franklin as minister to France. Jefferson quickly became enamored of all things French. "Were I to proceed to tell you how much I enjoy their architecture, sculpture, painting, music, I should

BOTANICALS

"I cultivate in my own garden here Indian corn for the use of my own table, to eat green in our manner," he wrote Nicholas Lewis in 1787 of his Paris home. He asked Lewis to send him watermelon, cantaloupe, and sweet potato seeds to share with Europeans. In return, his French friends gave him grapevines and other plants. Madame de Tessé later sent Jefferson this "golden-rain tree" (*Koelreuteria paniculatta*) for Monticello, the first of its type planted in America.

86

CRATES

of goods were shipped to Jefferson from France.

HOME FURNISHINGS

Jefferson kept a record of his purchases in Paris to furnish his house near the Champs-Élysées, including candlesticks, carpets, kitchen utensils, silver flatware, and at least 48 chairs, including this Louis XVI–era armchair. He asked Abigail Adams, at the time stationed in London with her husband John, to send him napkins and a tablecloth large enough for 20 people. Jefferson frequently entertained.

so ask the traveled inhabitant of any nation, In what country on earth would you rather live? . . . France." —Thomas Jefferson

want words," he wrote. Jefferson initially brought with him his 11-year-old daughter, Patsy, and 19-year-old slave James Hemings, whom he wanted to learn French cooking. They were later joined by 8-year-old Polly Jefferson and 14-year-old slave Sally Hemings. For most of his five years in Paris, Jefferson lived at the elegant Hôtel de Langeac to represent his new nation appropriately. ✦

JEFFERSON PORTRAIT BY HOUDON

Jean-Antoine Houdon's portrait is one of the best and best known likenesses of Jefferson. He considered Houdon the greatest sculptor of the age and sat for him in his Paris studio in 1789. The terra-cotta patinated plaster bust, now owned by Monticello, was shown in the Salon at the Louvre later that year. The plaster displayed by Jefferson at Monticello is lost. This likeness served as the model for the profile of Jefferson on the nickel first minted in 1943.

GIFT OF THE
GILDER LEHRMAN
COLLECTION

✳ THE PEOPLE

Maria Cosway

Jefferson was enchanted by Maria Cosway, an artist and musician, the moment he met her in Paris in 1786. He was a 43-year-old widower, and traveled around Paris visiting sites related to the arts with an intimate circle of friends that included the 27-year-old Maria, her husband, miniaturist Richard Cosway, and the American painter John Trumbull. After Maria left Paris later that year, Jefferson penned a love letter to her—the only such letter in his vast collection of correspondence—in which he describes her as having "qualities & accomplishments . . . such as music, modesty, beauty, & that softness of disposition which is the ornament of her sex & charm of ours."

ENGRAVING OF MARIA
COSWAY BY RICHARD
COSWAY, CA 1785

5

YEARS
The length of Jefferson's stay in Paris, from 1784 to 1789

COFFEE URN

Jefferson designed this "silver coffee pot" made by Parisian silversmith Jacques-Louis-Auguste Leguay in 1789. He was so fond of the 13¼-inch-tall urn he asked another silversmith to make a duplicate as a gift for architect Charles-Louis Clerisseau, who had helped Jefferson with plans for the Virginia State Capitol. Jefferson brought this urn back to Monticello with him.

Monticello II

JEFFERSON BEGAN PLANNING the major renovation and expansion of his home in 1790, the year after he returned to America from France. He was inspired by the architecture he saw in Paris, especially the Hôtel de Salm, with which he was "violently smitten." Construction of Monticello II began in 1796, when the cellars were excavated and the pillars on the northeast facade were removed. Skilled craftsmen trained and directed the work of Jefferson's slaves, who learned to be stonecutters, glaziers, and woodworkers. The roof was removed from most of the original house in the winter of 1798, and the iconic dome (the first on a private building in America) was completed in 1800. Jefferson directed construction from afar during the eight years he served as president and lived in Washington, D.C. Monticello II was largely finished in 1809, when Jefferson returned to his home in retirement.

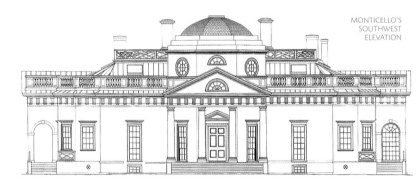

MONTICELLO'S
SOUTHWEST
ELEVATION

✴ THE HOUSE

Thomas Jefferson Foundation

Founded in 1923, the Thomas Jefferson Memorial Foundation was created with the stated purpose "to purchase, preserve, and maintain Monticello as a memorial to Thomas Jefferson and his ideals." Later that year, the Foundation achieved the first of those goals by acquiring Monticello from Jefferson Monroe Levy, nephew of Uriah P. Levy. (An advertisement of the sale is shown at right.) Repairs to the house and grounds began in 1924, and visitors were invited; that year 20,091 people paid $0.50 admission to view Monticello. The Foundation has continually increased the area of Jefferson's land under its care, from the initial 650 acres purchased in 1923 to approximately 2,500 acres after the 2004 purchase of neighboring Montalto.

1809

THE YEAR MONTICELLO II
was mostly finished, and Jefferson
returned from Washington, D.C.

*"We are none of us in very good
spirits just now owing to the
probability there is of Monticello
being sold"* —Cornelia Jefferson Randolph

✳ THE PEOPLE

Uriah P. Levy

The most important owners of Monticello,
other than the Jefferson family, were a U.S.
Navy commodore named Uriah Phillips Levy
and his nephew Jefferson Monroe Levy.
If Uriah hadn't purchased and cared for
Monticello when he did, it's quite possible
that Jefferson's house might not have with-
stood the ravages of time.

Born in Philadelphia to Jewish parents,
his mother of Portuguese ancestry, Uriah
Levy enlisted in the Navy, fought in the
Barbary Wars and the War of 1812, eventually
commanding the Mediterranean Squadron
and achieving the highest rank of the
time, commodore.

An admirer of Jefferson, Levy commis-
sioned the first public statue of him in 1832.
Upon learning that Monticello was in grave
disrepair and its owner eager to sell the property, Levy agreed in 1834 to purchase the
house and surrounding 218 acres of land for
$2,700 and began work to repair the damage.
For the renovation he employed a large
number of workers, among them more than
a dozen slaves he purchased, and personally
supervised the work during the first few years.

Levy's mother Rachel Phillips Levy, who
died in 1839, was buried along Mulberry Row.

By 1853 Levy's efforts had returned much
of Monticello's original glory in what was
arguably the first effort of historic preservation in America. An article in *Harper's New
Monthly Magazine* reported that the outside
of the house in general appearance was
"the same as when Jefferson left it." It also
noted that the parlor's parquet floor was
"polished like a table."

AFTER URIAH LEVY (ABOVE) DIED IN 1862, MONTICELLO
WAS TIED UP IN LENGTHY LITIGATION. JEFFERSON
MONROE LEVY PURCHASED THE PROPERTY IN 1879.

MONTICELLO FELL INTO DISREPAIR
DURING THE YEARS THAT URIAH
LEVY'S WILL WAS DISPUTED.
BEGINNING IN 1879, HIS NEPHEW
JEFFERSON MONROE LEVY DEVOTED
HIMSELF TO MONTICELLO'S CARE.

Before Your Visit

Jefferson owned nearly 9,000
books during his lifetime and
spent hours reading every day.

Planning Your Visit

BEFORE OR AFTER taking the shuttle to the Jefferson's mountaintop home, visitors of all ages can experience Jefferson's life and times at the David M. Rubenstein Visitor Center and the Carl and Hunter Smith Education Center. The visually rich introductory film *Thomas Jefferson's World* reveals Monticello's central role in Jefferson's life. Discover how the world reacted to the Declaration of Independence in the interactive digital exhibition, "The Boisterous Sea of Liberty." Explore the conditions of home life for slaves living on Mulberry Row in a reproduction log cabin designed for young visitors to the Griffin Discovery Room. A relief model in the courtyard shows the extent of the 5,000-acre plantation. Lunch or a snack may be purchased in the Café, and visitors can browse books and items for sale in the Shop at Monticello.

35

MINUTES

The approximate length of the house tour

364

DAYS A YEAR

Monticello is open every day except Christmas.

"...few know the Thomas Jefferson of Monticello." —*Thomas Jefferson's World*

DAVID M. RUBENSTEIN VISITOR CENTER AND CARL AND HUNTER SMITH EDUCATION CENTER

The starting point for your Monticello journey features interactive exhibitions about Jefferson's life and ideas, a hands-on discovery room for children, classrooms for educational programs, a theater, a café, the Shop at Monticello, and more.

✳ THE HOUSE

Tours of the House and Grounds

House: The property is open every day but Christmas. Hours vary seasonally; check *monticello.org* for details. The Day Pass includes a guided tour of Monticello's first floor. The Behind the Scenes tour includes the upstairs, including the iconic Dome Room. Other specialized tours are available.

Gardens and Grounds: Guided tours are offered of the gardens and landscape, April through October. The Slavery at Monticello tour is a guided tour of the life and work of Monticello's enslaved families. The Revolutionary Garden tour is an experiential tour of the vegetable garden and orchards.

For Kids: There are family-friendly tours for kids ages 6 to 12 seasonally. The Griffin Discovery Room contains interactive exhibits, and the Mountaintop Hands-on Activity Center includes quill pen writing, games, and more.

Special Events: Experience the Independence Day Celebration and Naturalization Ceremony, the Heritage Harvest Festival in September, and Holiday Evening Tours in December. For a complete list of events, visit *monticello.org/calendar*.

ENRICH YOUR MONTICELLO EXPERIENCE WITH A FREE APP (FOR IOS AND ANDROID DEVICES) THAT BRINGS JEFFERSON'S PLANTATION HOME TO LIFE. VISIT *MONTICELLO.ORG/APP* FOR DETAILS.

Rubenstein Visitor Center and Smith Education Center

THE IDEAL STARTING point for your journey is the David M. Rubenstein Visitor Center and Smith Education Center, the 21st-century gateway to Jefferson's timeless Monticello. Innovative exhibitions, resources for young people, and a powerful introductory film prepare visitors for their trip to the mountaintop, presenting fresh perspectives on Jefferson's life and the enduring significance of his ideas. In the courtyard near the Café, a 9.5-foot-by-5.5-foot bronze relief scale model of the 5,000-acre plantation reveals the mountaintop and the expansive property beyond it; a life-size statue of Jefferson greets visitors at the shuttle bus stop. In the Shop at Monticello (at right), visitors will find some 250 books, posters and prints, historic seeds, and more to browse and buy. Special events can be scheduled in the Robert H. and Clarice Smith Woodland Pavilion nestled in the white oak forest just beyond the Visitor Center.

MUSEUM EXHIBITIONS

SHUTTLE BUS TO MONTICELLO

ROBERT H. AND CLARICE SMITH GALLERY

JEFFERSON STATUE

THE SHOP AT MONTICELLO

DAVID M. RUBENSTEIN VISITOR CENTER

SHOP AT MONTICELLO

Gifts, gourmet foods and wines, and collectibles are available in the Shop at Monticello, which also features a special section for gardeners.

ROBERT H. AND CLARICE SMITH WOODLAND PAVILION

CAFÉ

HOWARD AND ABBY MILSTEIN THEATER

GRIFFIN DISCOVERY ROOM

DOMINION WELCOME PAVILION

CARL AND HUNTER SMITH EDUCATION CENTER

Robert H. and Clarice Smith Gallery

THE TWO-LEVEL, 5,200-square-foot Gallery houses four interactive exhibitions that offer Monticello's visitors an exciting new approach to the power and consequence of Thomas Jefferson's words and ideas. Through a groundbreaking presentation that includes a wall of flat-panel LCD screens, smaller touchable screens, and quotations projected on the floor, they explore Jefferson's dedication to his country, his radical ideas about liberty that changed the world, and his designs for Monticello—his home, plantation, and laboratory. The Gallery is accessible from both the courtyard and upper (shuttle bus station) levels.

MAKING MONTICELLO

Monticello was always a work in process. Jefferson began leveling the mountaintop in 1768 and didn't finish the West Portico columns until 1823. The exhibit "Making Monticello: Jefferson's 'Essay in Architecture,'" in the David Bruce Smith Gallery, explores Monticello's architectural origins, construction, and evolution. Visitors see Jefferson's innovative, evolving designs over time and learn about some of the enslaved and free workers and their trades that helped make his vision a reality.

"TO TRY ALL THINGS"

Monticello was the laboratory where Jefferson tested his theory that "useful knowledge" could make life more efficient and convenient. "Monticello as Experiment: 'To Try All Things'" features more than 200 objects from Monticello's permanent collection (including archaeological artifacts) to illustrate Jefferson's love of science and technology; his lifelong quest for knowledge; his innovative (if not always successful) approaches to agriculture, labor, industry, and design; and people who helped implement his ideas.

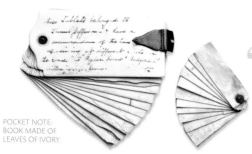

POCKET NOTE-
BOOK MADE OF
LEAVES OF IVORY.

" *His general abilities are
such as would do honor
to any age or Country.*"

—Nathaniel Cutting

"THE WORDS OF THOMAS JEFFERSON"

Here visitors will find an exhibition where Jefferson's thoughts literally come to light in a high-tech display. The broad scope of Jefferson's ideas are captured in words, such as "America," "Liberty," "Monticello," and "Rights," that are inlaid into the blue-stone floor. When visitors step near a word, key phrases are projected in light at their feet until the full quotation moves across the floor and is projected on a wall.

186

QUOTATIONS

appear in the exhibition "The Words of Thomas Jefferson."

"THE BOISTEROUS SEA OF LIBERTY"

A wall of flat-panel LCD monitors and seven interactive touch screens in "The Boisterous Sea of Liberty" exhibition trace the development and ongoing influence of Jefferson's transformational ideas about liberty—particularly those expressed in the Declaration of Independence. Beginning with the notion of liberty as it was understood in the British Empire in the 18th century, the exhibition charts how the ideas in the declaration shaped the government of the new United States and ultimately spread around the globe.

Griffin Discovery Room

AT THE GRIFFIN DISCOVERY ROOM, located on the lower level of the Smith Education Center, visitors are greeted by a life-size cutout of Thomas Jefferson, inviting them to "Discover the world of Monticello," and asking "What was it like to live and work here 200 years ago?" This educational environment provides a variety of ways for young people, especially those ages 6 to 12, to connect with Jefferson and the members of the larger Monticello community, and to learn what life was like for children in the early 1800s. Young visitors can even try on 18th-century costumes. Some of the activities include: assembling a chair similar to those from the era, operating a bellows to stoke a fire, adding ingredients to a pot hanging in a fireplace hearth, and making a rubbing of the words on Jefferson's tombstone. The Griffin Discovery Room is open daily.

HAWKINS & PEALE'S PATENT POLYGRAPH NO. 57 IS DISPLAYED IN JEFFERSON'S CABINET.

20+

HANDS-ON ACTIVITIES
are in the Griffin Discovery Room.

REPRODUCTION ELEMENTS

At the Griffin Discovery Room, visitors are encouraged to pick up, inspect, and use reproductions of many of the items in Jefferson's house. The space features reproduction elements from the Monticello house, such as Jefferson's alcove bed and Houdon's bust of Jefferson. Reproductions of plantation items and buildings include the nail-making shop and a slave dwelling. Children and their family members can write a letter (while making a copy) on a polygraph machine based on the one Jefferson owned. They can learn how to weave, touch a mastodon's jawbone, create secret codes on a wheel cipher based on Jefferson's design, play games popular in Jefferson's era, and more.

This room is not just for children. Who tours the house without wanting to touch the polygraph machine? Not me."

—Amy Jeffries, Thomas Jefferson Foundation

LOG DWELLING

Visitors can walk inside the kind of structure that many Monticello slaves would have lived in. The building suggests the five log dwellings located on Mulberry Row in 1796, which ranged in size from 12 feet by 14 feet to 12 feet by 20 feet. They were occupied primarily by household workers and artisans who worked on Mulberry Row.

150

YEARS

is how long the U.S. military used Jefferson's cipher.

JEFFERSON'S WHEEL CIPHER, LIKE THIS REPLICA, WAS USED FOR ENCODING MESSAGES.

EXPLORE
Hands-on activities show what Monticello was like in the early 1800s.

PLAY
Try out replicas of games that were popular in Jefferson's era.

DISCOVER
Use working reproductions of many gadgets found in the Monticello house.

African-American Graveyard

MEN, WOMEN, AND CHILDREN of Monticello's African-American families are buried in more than 40 graves in a wooded plot adjacent to the visitors parking area. During the winter of 2000–2001, archaeologists identified this site as a slave burial ground, confirming 20 graves, including those of eight children. Five of the graves have uninscribed field-stones at the head and foot; the rest have no surviving markers. Although the names of Monticello's enslaved residents are known, it has not been possible to identify the individuals buried here. No graves were disturbed in the course of the archaeological investigations.

to Monticello
⅓ mile

Jefferson-era road

N

0   25
FEET

◯ Depression

☐ Five-foot
  excavation square

↬ Grave shaft

Remembrance

African-American graveyards are considered the first black institu-tions in North America, and were expressions of the separateness slavery created. This burial ground is a sacred space reinforcing the human ties that bound together the members of Monticello's enslaved families. Other slave burial sites on the 5,000-acre Monticello planta-tion have not yet been located.

Saunders-Monticello Trail

BEGINNING AT KEMPER PARK at the base of the Thomas Jefferson Parkway (Virginia State Route 53), the two-mile Saunders-Monticello Trail winds its way up the side of Carter Mountain. It runs through native hardwood forest and across deep ravines, offering spectacular views of the Blue Ridge Mountains. After crossing the stone-arch Saunders Bridge, the trail leads directly to the Rubenstein Visitor Center and Smith Education Center. Constructed partly of raised boardwalk and partly of finely crushed packed stone, the trail is open to pedestrians, cyclists, and to those in wheelchairs. Dogs are welcome in the Kemper Park section, and must be on a leash. The trail is open all year from sunrise to sunset.

11

TRAILS
make up the Thomas Jefferson Parkway hiking trails.

TRAIL TREASURES
Birds frequent the trail's arboretum with its trees and shrubs from across Albemarle County.

The House

Nestled in the hills surrounding
Charlottesville, Virginia,
Monticello is a fine example
of Roman neoclassicism.

First Impressions

FOLLOWING HIS VISIT TO JEFFERSON'S home in 1782, the Marquis de Chastellux wrote that "it shines alone in this secluded spot." Jefferson might have been pleased by this description. He had carefully designed Monticello (which means "little mountain") to elevate American taste. Many visual cues, from the mansion's location on a mountaintop to the original style of the building, convey a sense of Jefferson's aspirations and knowledge. His influence touched every room inside Monticello as well. In the Hall, with its cavernous 18-foot-tall ceiling, he displayed artwork and artifacts that could only have been collected by someone with his intellectual curiosity. The Hall made a powerful impression upon visitors, who were often dazzled by his collection. Nearly 250 years later, visitors are still awed by their first glimpse of Jefferson's masterpiece.

HOUSE FACADE
The house's L-shaped wings conceal the work spaces built into the mountaintop.

NORTH PAVILION

WEST FACADE

" *my essay in Architecture . . .* "

—Thomas Jefferson

CHARLES WILLSON
PEALE PAINTED
THIS PORTRAIT
OF JEFFERSON AT
AGE 48 IN 1791.

CLIMBING THE MOUNTAIN

Jefferson loved Monticello's lofty location and the sweeping views it afforded
from the windows and grounds, but
many guests were less than fond of
the challenging ascent to the 867-foot
mountaintop. Travelers using the most
common route, called the East Road, had
to cross the Rivanna River before reach-
ing the base of the mountain. From there
some found it safer to continue up the
road on foot rather than on horseback
or in their carriages. During an 1815 visit,
scholar George Ticknor compared the
journey to another climb: "The ascent
of this steep, savage hill, was as pensive
and slow as Satan's ascent to Paradise."

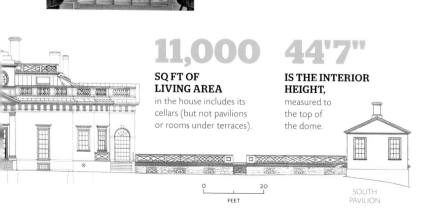

11,000
SQ FT OF
LIVING AREA
in the house includes its
cellars (but not pavilions
or rooms under terraces).

44'7"
IS THE INTERIOR
HEIGHT,
measured to
the top of
the dome.

0   20
FEET

SOUTH
PAVILION

House Plans

THIS CROSS SECTION shows Monticello after the expansion between 1796 and 1809. Architectural elements such as the dome, skylights, narrow stairs, and bed alcoves reflect ideas Jefferson brought back from France.

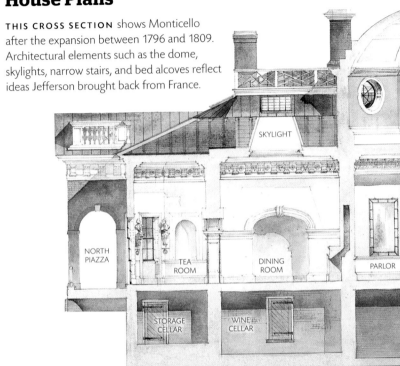

SKYLIGHT

NORTH PIAZZA

TEA ROOM

DINING ROOM

PARLOR

STORAGE CELLAR

WINE CELLAR

✳ THE HOUSE

Rooms for Living

Monticello's design reflects the house's function as both a plantation headquarters and a home for Jefferson and his family. He frequently entertained close friends like James and Dolley Madison, occasional foreign dignitaries such as the Marquis de Lafayette and Abbé Corrêa da Serra, and numerous uninvited guests eager to meet the retired president. Visitors were received in "public" rooms—the Hall, Parlor, Dining Room, and Tea Room—while the private spaces were reserved for the family. Jefferson's suite of rooms, called his "sanctum sanctorum" by one guest, indicates how private it was.

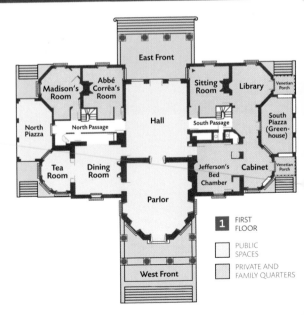

East Front

Madison's Room

Abbé Corrêa's Room

Sitting Room

Library

Venetian Porch

North Piazza

North Passage

Hall

South Passage

South Piazza (Greenhouse)

Tea Room

Dining Room

Jefferson's Bed Chamber

Cabinet

Venetian Porch

Parlor

West Front

1 FIRST FLOOR

PUBLIC SPACES

PRIVATE AND FAMILY QUARTERS

"Architecture . . . is then among the most important arts: and it is desireable to introduce taste into an art which shews so much." —Thomas Jefferson

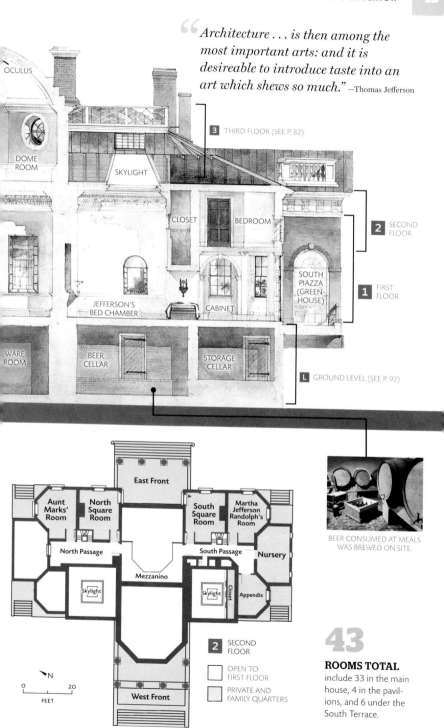

OCULUS

DOME ROOM

SKYLIGHT

3 THIRD FLOOR (SEE. P. 82)

CLOSET   BEDROOM

2 SECOND FLOOR

SOUTH PIAZZA (GREEN-HOUSE)

1 FIRST FLOOR

JEFFERSON'S BED CHAMBER

CABINET

WARE ROOM

BEER CELLAR

STORAGE CELLAR

L GROUND LEVEL (SEE. P. 92)

East Front

Aunt Marks' Room

North Square Room

South Square Room

Martha Jefferson Randolph's Room

North Passage

South Passage

Nursery

Mezzanino

Skylight

Skylight

Closet

Appendix

2 SECOND FLOOR

☐ OPEN TO FIRST FLOOR

☐ PRIVATE AND FAMILY QUARTERS

N

0   20
FEET

West Front

BEER CONSUMED AT MEALS WAS BREWED ON SITE.

43

ROOMS TOTAL include 33 in the main house, 4 in the pavilions, and 6 under the South Terrace.

East Front

WHEN APPROACHING MONTICELLO, whether in Jefferson's time or today, most people's first glimpse of Jefferson's house is this view of the East Front. Visitors entered the house through the Northeast Portico, passing under the weather vane and the exterior face of the Great Clock and into the entrance area, which Jefferson referred to as the Hall.

CHINESE GONG

To signal each hour on the Great Clock, Jefferson's workmen installed a 22-inch-diameter Chinese-made gong on the Northeast Portico roof. "I wish for one to serve as the bell to a clock, which might be heard all over my farm...," he wrote to a friend.

" *when we consider how much climate contributes to the happiness of our condition, by the fine sensations it excites, & the productions it is the parent of, we have reason to value highly the accident of birth in . . . Virginia.*" —Thomas Jefferson

✳ THE HOUSE

Weather Vane Inside and Out

The arrow on this compass on the Northeast Portico's ceiling is connected to the weather vane on the roof directly above. For Jefferson, weather was a lifelong passion. He recorded detailed observations of temperature and precipitation and, despite inadequate measuring devices, attempted to collect data on humidity and wind speed. When Lewis and Clark set out on their westward journey in 1803, Jefferson asked that they observe "climate as characterized by the thermometer, by the proportion of rainy, cloudy & clear days, by lightening, hail, snow, ice . . ." Jefferson has been claimed by the National Weather Service as the "father of weather observers."

West Front

THE SOUTHWEST PORTICO, topped by Monticello's iconic dome, is at the center of the symmetrical West Front. Designed as an extension of the Parlor's living space, the portico offered cooling shade during the summer months and views of the elaborate garden. Today new U.S. citizens are sworn in on the West Portico steps every Independence Day.

NICKEL IMAGE
Updated in 2006, the U.S. nickel coin shows the Southwest Portico in greater detail than the 1938 version.

GUTTAE
More than 3,800 of these small circular details are included in the Doric entablature around the house exterior.

DOORWAY
This doorway, used by family and guests, provides access between the Parlor and the West Lawn.

14

**PAIRS OF
WINDOW SASHES**
sent from England
likely included
glazed windows.

*I am as happy no where else & in
no other society, & all my wishes
end, where I hope my days will end,
at Monticello."* —Thomas Jefferson

✳ THE HOUSE

Why Are the Columns Tan?

Does something look different on Monticello's famous
West Front? Look closely and you'll see the Doric columns of the Southwest Portico are tan, not white. The
columns are tan because their curved "compass" bricks
were coated with a stuccolike "rendering" that makes
them look like stone. Experts recently removed more
than 20 coats of white paint and restored the columns'
surfaces to their original appearance.

The Dome

JEFFERSON ADMIRED THE new buildings of Paris during his five years there as minister to France, writing that "I was violently smitten with the Hôtel de Salm, and used to go to the Thuileries almost daily to look at it." Its domed roof, along with the dome of the Halle au Blé (grain market), led him to incorporate a dome into his expansion of Monticello, making it the first domed residence in America.

INSPIRATION
Jefferson was impressed by the dome of the Hôtel de Salm in Paris.

TEMPLE OF VESTA, ROME, *THE ARCHITECTURE OF A. PALLADIO*, GIACOMO LEONI

8

CIRCULAR WINDOWS provide natural light in the Dome Room.

OCULUS: GLASS SKYLIGHT IN CROWN OF DOME

HONEYCOMBED ROOF

Jefferson's design for Monticello's dome (above) was also influenced by the Temple of Vesta in Rome and the spectacular skylighted Halle au Blé, the new Paris grain market by architects Legrand and Molinos. Jefferson was intrigued by the dome's visible supporting ribs. They divided the dome into sections small enough to hold glass panes that illuminated the market.

When Jefferson turned to the construction of Monticello's dome in 1800, he consulted a book by 16th-century French architect Philibert Delorme. Jefferson simplified Delorme's complicated joinery of mortises, tenons, and wooden keys by substituting laminated sections fastened with nails made in his plantation nailery. Ever the mathematician, Jefferson adjusted the dome's design to fit it onto the existing irregular octagon room (left).

How Monticello Was Built

JEFFERSON, A SELF-TAUGHT ARCHITECT, described Monticello as "my essay in Architecture." Like his other famous essay, the Declaration of Independence, it underwent significant revision before it was finished. With his first design, begun in 1768, he rejected buildings that demonstrated little understanding of architectural principles and instead relied on the illustrations of ancient Roman architecture and Renaissance designs published by Andrea Palladio. The second design—today's Monticello—also was influenced by buildings he admired in France. In 1823, three years before his death, the West Portico's Doric columns were finally completed.

10

VERTICAL FEET of dirt and rock were removed from the mountain summit to prepare the house site.

CARPENTRY AND JOINERY TOOLS

THE SOUTH PAVILION WAS MONTICELLO'S FIRST BUILDING.

THEODOLITE
This sophisticated surveying instrument measured both horizontal and vertical angles.

CONSTRUCTION TIME LINE

1768	Leveling work begins on Monticello mountaintop.
1770	South Pavilion is completed.
1771	Construction begins on Monticello I.
1770s	Jefferson acquires adjacent mountain, names it Montalto (high mountain).
1778	Monticello I brickwork is completed.
1784	Work is suspended when Jefferson departs for France.
1796	Construction begins on Monticello II.
1800	Dome is constructed.
1803	Jefferson designs innovative "zigzag" roof.
1805	Interior painting begins, decorative floors are installed.
1809	Monticello II is largely completed as Jefferson begins retirement.
1823	Doric columns complete West Portico.

◄ THE PEOPLE

Who Built Monticello

Preparation for construction began in 1768 with the clearing and leveling of the mountaintop. Jefferson then hired a neighbor's slaves to dig the cellars. His architectural vision for Monticello would not have been achieved without hired white artisans who trained their enslaved assistants. Jefferson's records identify the names of 69 free and enslaved brickmakers, bricklayers, blacksmiths, carpenters, joiners, glaziers, nailmakers, painters, plasterers, roofers, sawyers, and stonemasons.

James Dinsmore, an Irish joiner, headed the construction of Monticello II from 1798 to 1809. Jefferson wrote that Dinsmore was one of the "more faithful, sober, discreet, honest and respectable men I have ever known." Dinsmore, who made much of the intricate woodwork inside the house, trained John Hemmings, who succeeded him as head joiner in 1809. Hemmings, described by an overseer as "a first-rate workman," erected log buildings on Mulberry Row, architectural woodwork in the house, and fine furniture, including a special desk for Ellen Randolph Coolidge, Jefferson's granddaughter.

The Hall

TO EDUCATE VISITORS AS they entered Monticello, Jefferson created a two-story museum with a distinctly American focus. Maps, copies of old master paintings, busts of French thinkers, and natural history specimens conveyed his interest in the larger world. Antlers, including those of moose, deer, elk, and American bighorn sheep, as well as mastodon fossils found in Kentucky, were displayed as examples of the New World's indigenous wildlife. Native American "tokens of friendship," sent back from the Lewis and Clark expedition to the Northwest, composed what Jefferson called "a kind of Indian Hall."

JEFFERSON'S WAITING ROOM

Visitors were a frequent occurrence at Monticello, sometimes in abundance: Jefferson's daughter Martha recalled the house being besieged by as many as 50 guests at a time. To accommodate such an influx, 28 chairs were placed in the Hall, creating an area for guests to wait before being received by their host. Some visitors were lucky enough to be given a firsthand history lesson from Jefferson, who liked to describe the people and events depicted in Asher B. Durand's engraving of John Trumbull's "Declaration of Independence of the United States of America," which hung over the fireplace.

ALEXANDER HAMILTON
Jefferson placed the marble bust of political opponent opposite his ow
This is a copy of the 1794 original I
Italian sculptor Giuseppe Cerac

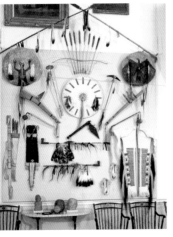

REPRODUCTIONS OF NATIVE AMERICAN ARTIFACTS FROM LEWIS AND CLARK EXPEDITION, 1804–1806

MASTODON JAW EXCAVATED IN BIG BONE LICK, KENTUCKY, 1807

ELK ANTLERS SENT TO
JEFFERSON BY LEWIS
AND CLARK, 1805

Great Clock

Besides displaying the time of day, Jefferson's ingenious clock also indicated the days of the week as its weights descended on ropes past markers on the wall. The clock is connected to a Chinese gong on the roof that strikes the hours. A second clock face on the exterior East Front wall displayed the hours. When Jefferson discovered that Monticello's ceiling was not tall enough for the clock, rather than recalibrate it, his workmen cut a hole in the floor to allow the weights to descend all the way to the Saturday marker in the basement.

18'6"

TALL CEILING

Impressive with two stories, the Hall greets visitors to Monticello, as in Jefferson's day.

NATIVE AMERICAN SHIELD

This replica of an artifact Jefferson owned was created at United Tribes Technical College, in Bismarck, North Dakota.

CLOCK
WEIGHTS

Family Sitting Room

ORIGINALLY PART OF JEFFERSON'S PRIVATE SUITE and called the Book Room, it became a family sitting room only after the sale of his books to Congress. Martha Jefferson Randolph, Jefferson's oldest daughter, regularly used it as a classroom when teaching her children. Jefferson modified the room's Rumford fireplace (below), specially designed to radiate heat from burning wood rather than coal, making it one of the easiest rooms in the house to keep warm.

8
TOTAL FIREPLACES
burned wood to heat the house, as did two stoves on the main floor.

HOUSEWIFE
Martha Jefferson Randolph's red leather needle case, or "housewife," doubled as a diary. She kept it handy for mending and note-taking.

SEWING TABLE
For Martha Jefferson Randolph and her daughters, as well as for enslaved women, sewing clothes and mending was a never-ending job. This table, with a deep drawer to hold sewing projects, was made in Monticello's joiner's shop.

"MONTICELLO FROM EDGEHILL," PAINTED BY CORNELIA J. RANDOLPH

✳ THE PEOPLE

12
CHILDREN
were born to Martha Jefferson Randolph from 1791 to 1818, including Cornelia (right).

Cornelia Jefferson Randolph
The fifth child of Jefferson's daughter Martha and her husband Thomas Mann Randolph, Cornelia grew up at Monticello and learned about architecture from her grandfather. She practiced by sketching his designs for the University of Virginia. Jefferson described Cornelia and her sister Ellen in a letter to their mother from Poplar Forest as "the severest students I have ever met with. They never leave their room but to come to meals." Cornelia drew a floor plan of Monticello, noting the location of many furnishings and artworks, and providing important clues about how the house was arranged.

Library

THIS WAS ONE OF FOUR SPACES—along with the Greenhouse, Cabinet, and Bed Chamber—that make up Jefferson's private suite, dubbed his "sanctum sanctorum" by a friend from Washington. In 1814, just after the British burned the U.S. Capitol and the nation's fledgling library, Jefferson "ceded" (he never called it a "sale") his collection to Congress as a replacement. Covering a wide variety of subjects, his books became the nucleus of the Library of Congress. Jefferson began a new library to enjoy during retirement, amassing some 2,000 favorite books. The Library is also where Jefferson drew his plans for the University of Virginia.

THE SCREW PRESS WAS USED FOR FLATTENING TIGHTLY FOLDED LETTERS.

SLIPCOVERS PROTECTED THE UPHOLSTERY ON THESE FRENCH ARMCHAIRS.

SORTED MAIL COULD BE KEPT SAFELY LOCKED IN THIS OCTAGONAL TABLE.

" *I cannot live without books . . .*" —Thomas Jefferson

FAMILY COPY OF OVID'S *METAMORPHOSES*,
1568. JEFFERSON STUDIED THE CLASSICS
THROUGHOUT HIS LIFE

ASTRONOMICAL CLOCK

An 1811 solar eclipse inspired Jefferson to order a clock "as good as hands can make it" to record astronomical observations.

THE ADJUSTABLE TABLE
WAS IDEALLY SUITED
FOR DRAFTING.

£200

WORTH OF BOOKS
were lost when Shadwell, Jefferson's boyhood home, was destroyed by fire in 1770.

6,500

BOOKS WERE SOLD
to replace the congressional library that burned during the War of 1812.

✳ THE HOUSE

Greenhouse

A connection to nature was an essential part of Jefferson's sanctum sanctorum. Just off the Library, the Southeast Piazza functioned as a greenhouse where he grew orange, acacia, and lime trees. The room also served as an aviary for his pet mockingbirds, and as a workshop for making locks and chains. The floor-to-ceiling double-sashed windows acted as doorways, providing access to the South Terrace as well as to the East and West Fronts.

Jefferson's Eye for Detail

Entablatures and Friezes

JEFFERSON FILLED MONTICELLO'S rooms with artworks and objects that were useful to him, including a variety of conveniences. Visitors today often remember such novel features as the parquet floor and double-acting door in the Parlor or the alcove bed joining the Bed Chamber and Cabinet. But look up in many rooms and you will discover some of Jefferson's most elaborate architectural details—the entablatures.

THE JUPITER FRIEZE
Rimming the Parlor ceiling, the "Jupiter Frieze" was based on Rome's Temple of Jupiter the Thunderer and depicts ox skulls, urns, and other symbols of sacrifice.

BED CHAMBER FRIEZE
The ox skulls, swags, candelabra, and *putti* (images of children) in Jefferson's Bed Chamber are based on the Temple of Fortuna Virilis in the Roman Forum. Jefferson referred to a drawing by Antoine Desgodetz, whose 1779 edition of *Les Édifices Antiques de Rome* provided detailed engravings of Roman monuments.

5,000+
GUTTAE, small wooden cones in rectangular groupings of 18, are part of the Doric entablatures around the Dining Room, Tea Room, and exterior.

"Roman taste, genius & magnificence excite ideas . . ." —Thomas Jefferson

Jefferson's designs for the entablatures and their decorative friezes were often based on those found in ancient buildings in or around Rome. The one in the Hall was based on details from the Corinthian Temple of Antoninus and Faustina in Rome. His Bed Chamber frieze features designs ranging from skulls to children, drawn from examples in the Roman Forum. Jefferson created a full-size drawing to guide craftsmen. ✼

DINING ROOM FRIEZE

The frieze in the Dining Room is decorated with alternating ornaments of rosettes and ox skulls made of "compo," a mixture of chalk, resin, glue, and oil that was pressed into molds. The surrounding woodwork was carved by skilled artisans, like James Dinsmore, the head joiner, who created many of the interior decorative touches.

PARTS OF AN ENTABLATURE

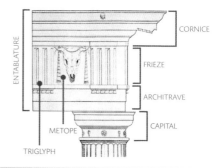

CORNICE

ENTABLATURE

FRIEZE

ARCHITRAVE

CAPITAL

METOPE

TRIGLYPH

HALL FRIEZE

The entablature in the Hall (above and right) features a frieze of the Ionic order. It is based on a drawing by Roland Fréart de Chambray in his book, *Parallèle de l'architecture antique avec la moderne*, the first complete translation into French of the works of Roman architect Vitruvius. Jefferson wrote "Hall" on a page that had designs by both Andrea Palladio and Vincenzo Scamozzi. As often was the case, Jefferson followed Palladio.

Cabinet

THE CABINET, JEFFERSON'S office space, was the nucleus of his intellectual and scientific world. Nestled in the heart of his "sanctum sanctorum," between the Library and his Bed Chamber, the Cabinet is where he kept up with his extensive correspondence (he received 1,267 letters in 1820 alone) and made detailed notes about the plantation in his "Farm Book" and "Garden Book." The Cabinet is where Jefferson enjoyed a daily nap on his sofa.

JOHN ADAMS BUST
This plaster copy of the 1818 original by J. B. Binon was a gift from Benjamin Gould in 1825.

THEODOLITE
(SEE PAGE 49)

TERRESTRIAL (LEFT) AND CELESTIAL GLOBES OFTEN CAME AS A PAIR.

35

SCIENTIFIC INSTRUMENTS,
and possibly more, were owned by Jefferson.

A ROOM OF TREASURES

Surrounded by devices and contraptions of all kinds, Jefferson was a gadget lover. His Cabinet was filled with telescopes, drafting and surveying equipment, and custom-made furniture such as his revolving stand and desk with adjustable top. The polygraph, a two-pen copying machine (below), created duplicates of some of the roughly 19,000 letters Jefferson wrote; these copies provide rich information about Jefferson's life.

CELESTIAL GLOBE

2

TIMES A DAY
Jefferson recorded outdoor temperature.

" from sun-rise to one or two aclock, and often from dinner to dark, I am drudging at the writing table." —Thomas Jefferson

WALLPAPER SAMPLES FROM A BOOK USED AT MONTICELLO

BAROMETER USED FOR WEATHER OBSERVATIONS

THE REVOLVING STAND CAN BE USED SEATED OR STANDING.

STRIAL ⊃BE

WAYWISER USED FOR MARKING OFF ACREAGE

JEFFERSON REHABILITATED HIS WRIST BY LIFTING THESE LEAD DUMBBELLS.

THE POLYGRAPH PRODUCED TWO LETTERS AT ONCE.

A FOLDING SCREEN SEPARATED THE CABINET FROM THE BED CHAMBER.

Jefferson's Bed Chamber

ALWAYS AN EARLY RISER, Jefferson is said to have claimed that "the sun had not caught him in bed for fifty years." Daniel Webster, during an 1824 visit to Monticello (when Jefferson was 81 years old), wrote that "Mr. Jefferson rises in the morning as soon as he can see the hands of his clock . . ." His morning routine included building his own fire and soaking his feet in cold water, which he credited for his good health. Jefferson used mirrors to maximize light from the opposite windows. The large skylight in the 18.5-foot-tall ceiling added more light. In a closetlike space at the foot of his bed, a rotating clothes rack with 48 arms kept his coats and waistcoats organized. The privy near his Bed Chamber was an example of early indoor facilities.

1 A CAMPECHE CHAIR SAT NEAR THE WINDOW IN THE SUMMER

2 FRENCH ARMCHAIRS OFFERED COMFORTABLE SEATING

3 CHEST OF DRAWERS OWNED BY MARTHA JEFFERSON

4 HUMBLE BOOKCASE MADE BY JEFFERSON

SPACE SAVERS

During the renovation of Monticello that began in the 1790s, Jefferson added space-saving alcove beds (left) to all of the new bedrooms, an arrangement he had seen in France. Since his Bed Chamber was in the existing part of the house, Jefferson widened the wall shared with his Cabinet to create the alcove. Jefferson died in this alcove on July 4, 1826.

Obelisk Clock

Jefferson had a lifelong fascination with obelisks, several of which he observed during his travels in Europe. While sketching the shape of a mantel clock to replace one that had been stolen, Jefferson incorporated the dual obelisks seen on this clock. He sent William Short, his secretary in Paris, the design sketch and detailed instructions about features he wanted the clockmaker to include. On the list were a pendulum, a second hand, and a chime to sound every hour and half hour.

VISITORS COMMENTED ON THE UNIQUE CLOTHES HORSE.

CAMPEACHY CHAIR BUILT
FROM MAHOGANY

CURTAINS WERE
MADE IN PHILADELPHIA
TO JEFFERSON'S
SPECIFICATIONS.

A PLACE FOR MUSIC

Jefferson called music the "favorite passion of [his] soul," an impressive statement given the range of his accomplishments, from architecture to horticulture. By his own estimation, he practiced playing the violin for more than 13,000 hours during his lifetime. It was a passion he shared with family and visitors in the Parlor, a room used for family time and entertaining. His daughters and granddaughters often filled the room with music, playing instruments such as the harpsichord and guitar (below).

HARPSICHORD

Jefferson advised
his daughter Martha
to practice the harpsichord
three hours a day. He
ordered one for her in 1786
from renowned London
maker Jacob Kirckman.

Parlor

EVENINGS AT MONTICELLO were often spent in the Parlor, where Jefferson and his family entertained guests with music, games, and conversation. When Jefferson returned from France in 1789, he brought 86 crates of goods purchased in Europe, many of which are found in this room, along with American furnishings. Martha Jefferson Randolph acquired the French armchairs seen here, made by cabinetmaker Georges Jacob, from her sister-in-law. More than 25 paintings line the walls. Jefferson designed the Parlor's double doors to open together when either side was moved. They still function, using the original mechanism from 1805.

A CAMERA OBSCURA, PRECURSOR TO THE MODERN CAMERA, PROJECTED IMAGES AND WAS OFTEN USED TO PRACTICE DRAWING.

29

PAINTINGS IN THE PARLOR included portraits of America's explorers and founders, and copies of old masters.

PAINTING FROM PARIS
Jefferson purchased "Herodias Bearing the Head of St. John the Baptist" in 1785.

CHESS SET
Jefferson's favorite board game was chess. This set was carved from ivory in the "barley corn" style, so called for the carved leaf designs on the kings and queens.

✳ THE HOUSE

Parquet Floor

Jefferson based the design of the parquet floor—a surface made from small pieces of wood arranged in a geometrical pattern—on a floor he saw in France. Like much of the elegant woodwork inside Monticello, the floor was the work of Irish head joiner James Dinsmore. When it was completed in 1806, the colors on the deep red cherry center squares contrasted with the lighter beech borders even more dramatically than they do today. One visitor observed that the floor was "kept polished as highly as if it were of fine mahogany."

Dining Room

AROUND 8 A.M. FOR BREAKFAST and 4 p.m. for dinner, enslaved butler Burwell Colbert rang a bell inviting family and guests into the Dining Room. To ensure that his cooks could prepare French cuisine, Jefferson took his slave James Hemings with him to France in 1784, and later brought two enslaved girls, Edith Fossett and Frances Hern, to train with a French chef at the President's House. Fruits, vegetables, and meats from the plantation were augmented by imported delicacies such as olive oil and Parmesan cheese. Around 1815 Jefferson painted the room in the fashionable "chrome yellow" seen on the walls today.

Hidden Features
(In service of conversation)

Many innovations in the Dining Room were designed with "a greater eye to convenience" and to limit disruptions. Several dumbwaiters, tiered trays on casters holding food, were placed near the dinner table to minimize the presence of servants, who might interrupt or eavesdrop on conversations. As guests finished their courses, used dishes were placed on the dumbwaiters' empty lower shelves. Wine was served at the end of the meal, Jefferson's favorite part, when he enjoyed the easy flow of after-dinner conversation. To facilitate wine service, two pulley-operated dumbwaiters hidden on either end of the fireplace could bring four bottles at a time up from the wine cellar.

FRENCH-STYLE DUMBWAITER

> *Dinner is served in half Virginian, half French style, in good taste & abundance."* —Daniel Webster

SILVER ASKOS, USED AS A CHOCOLATE POT, WHICH JEFFERSON HAD MODELED AFTER A ROMAN BRONZE POURING VESSEL EXCAVATED IN NÎMES, FRANCE

SILVER TUMBLER, TODAY CALLED A JEFFERSON CUP, ONE OF EIGHT JEFFERSON HAD MADE IN 1810

"A VIEW OF THE FALLS OF NIAGARA," ENGRAVING AFTER JOHN VANDERLYN, 1804

MAHOGANY SHIELD BACK ARMCHAIR

DOUBLE POCKET DOORS ON ROLLERS LEADING TO THE TEA ROOM

Highlights of Monticello's Collection

A taste for the finer things

AS MINISTER OF THE YOUNG American republic, Jefferson lived in Paris from 1784 to 1789. In France he learned to savor and cultivate that quality called "joie de vivre," enjoying good food, good wine, and good company. He acquired artworks, silver wares, painted porcelain, stylish armchairs, and other fine goods there. Jefferson also indulged in purchases during a trip with John Adams in 1786 to

SILVER GOBLETS

Jefferson engaged the silversmith Odiot to make two goblets, but it was another master, Claude-Nicolas Delanoy, who carried out the commission in 1789 based on Jefferson's own design. The goblets vary slightly in size and stem shape and cost 229 livres.

JEFFERSON-DESIGNED GOBLET, 1789

EDGEHILL PORTRAIT

The National Gallery of Art calls Gilbert Stuart "the most successful portraitist of early America," but Jefferson was less impressed by his customer service. It took 21 years (as well as intervention on Jefferson's behalf by former Secretary of War Henry Dearborn) for Stuart to deliver the painting, which later hung at Edgehill, the home of Jefferson's grandson.

SPECTACLES

At left are a silver case, spectacle frame, lenses in paper wrappers, and a set of green-tinted lens spectacles. According to Silvio Bedini, an expert in early scientific instruments, the spectacles were used "to improve the vision out of doors."

you see I am an enthusiast on the subject of the arts . . . to improve the taste of my countrymen, to increase their reputation, to reconcile to them the respect of the world & procure them it's praise." —Thomas Jefferson

England, where he picked up gloves, a hat, a walking stick, maps, and the best scientific instruments he could find. Taking a liking to the captain's "universal" table during his voyage back to America in 1789, he arranged for two just like it to be made for himself. ✺

FAUTEUIL EN CABRIOLET

In 1785 Jefferson moved into a spacious Paris townhouse called Hôtel de Langeac after his promotion to minister to France (succeeding Benjamin Franklin). When he returned to the United States, included in the furniture shipped from France were 48 chairs from at least three different suites. One of them, with a concave oval back, was the last chair in which Jefferson sat before he died (at left). In 1962, First Lady Jacqueline Kennedy purchased two similar fauteuils and used them in the West Sitting Room of the White House.

DRAFTING SET

These pocket-size instruments, likely purchased in 1786 from a store in London, would have provided Jefferson the tools needed to make measured drawings while traveling. In the diary he kept while in the Rhine Valley and the Netherlands, he frequently added sketches of buildings or maps.

100

DOLLARS

The fee Jefferson paid to Gilbert Stuart for the "Edgehill Portrait"

HOPE WITH CUPID

Made of an unglazed soft-paste porcelain called biscuit, these small sculptures were often found on 18th-century dining tables. Although Jefferson purchased ten or more such statuettes, only two are known today. "Hope With Cupid" dates to 1785 and was made at the renowned Sèvres porcelain factory in France.

DOUBLE POCKET
DOORS HELPED KEEP
COLD AIR FROM THE
TEA ROOM OUT
OF THE DINING
ROOM WITHOUT
LIMITING SUNLIGHT.

HENRY DEARBORN, JEFFERSON'S
SECRETARY OF WAR, SILHOUETTE BY
SAINT-MÉMIN, CIRCA 1805

FOUR VEGETABLE DISHES WERE
JEFFERSON'S MOST EXPENSIVE
PURCHASE OF FRENCH SILVER.

Tea Room

DESCRIBED BY JEFFERSON as his "most honorable suite," this room displayed likenesses of individuals who influenced both the American Revolution and Jefferson personally. Tea was popular at Monticello. Jefferson's letters and financial records indicate that he purchased "about 20 lb. of good tea annually" and preferred a green variety called Young Hyson. But the Tea Room served many more functions than the pouring of its namesake beverage. If guests outnumbered the Dining Room's seating capacity, the pocket doors could be opened and overflow diners seated here.

34

INFLUENTIAL FIGURES
are on display in the Tea Room, in sculptures and engravings.

MARQUIS DE LAFAYETTE

Jefferson purchased a bust of his trusted friend from Jean-Antoine Houdon in 1789. This is a copy of the plaster Jefferson owned.

SEAU CRÉNELÉ: FRENCH-MADE PORCELAIN CONTAINER USED TO RINSE AND COOL WINE GLASSES

DUMBWAITER AND COFFEE SERVICE

While in Paris, Jefferson adopted the European practice of using dumbwaiters, small sets of shelves, to simplify service before, during, and after a meal. Enslaved servants would likely set out food and drink in elegant tableware, such as this coffee service, in advance, and then would return after the meal. Jefferson continued using dumbwaiters while serving as president, and in retirement. This one was fashioned in the Monticello Joiner's Shop.

FORK AND TABLESPOON

One of Jefferson's first purchases in Paris was a set of 12 silver spoons and forks.

Living Indoors and Out

Terraces and Piazzas

MONTICELLO HAD LITTLE in common with contemporary Virginia plantation houses, including their tendency to be compact and focus on the interior. Jefferson embraced the use of outdoor areas as living spaces, both around the perimeter of the house and across the terraces extending to the pavilions. His goal was to make these areas as inviting and comfortable as possible by adding touches like louvers and shutters to provide shade and create

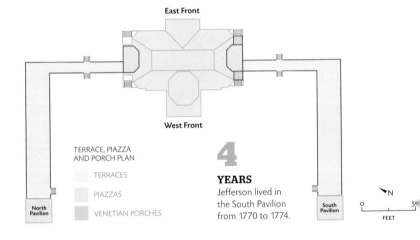

East Front

West Front

TERRACE, PIAZZA AND PORCH PLAN

TERRACES

PIAZZAS

VENETIAN PORCHES

North Pavilion

South Pavilion

4 YEARS
Jefferson lived in the South Pavilion from 1770 to 1774.

N

0 — 5

FEET

NORTH TERRACE

WEST VENETIAN PORCH

SOUTHEAST PIAZZA

EAST VENETIAN PORCH

CORNER OF SOUTH TERRACE LOOKING TOWARD JEFFERSON'S SUITE

" *I am . . . as exclusively employed out of doors as I was within doors when at Washington, and I find myself infinitely happier . . .*" —Thomas Jefferson

private spaces, which Jefferson valued. The outdoor spaces were used for taking walks after dinner, reading, conversation, enjoying the garden and vistas, and as places for grandchildren to run and play. They also added considerable area to the living space of the house, and would have been especially desirable during the summer months as an escape from the hot, stuffy indoor air. ❖

SPHERICAL SUNDIAL
Time is indicated by the position of an iron bar's shadow across vertical lines on the sphere.

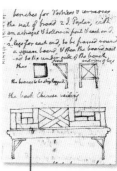

SOUTHEAST PIAZZA
As if to stress his connection to nature, every room in Jefferson's cherished "sanctum sanctorum"— his private suite that included his Bed Chamber, Cabinet, Library, and the Greenhouse (or Southeast Piazza)—has access points to the outside. In fact, the Southeast Piazza has three: a large triple sash window that opens onto the South Terrace, and doors at either end that lead to the east and west Venetian porches.

JEFFERSON DESIGNED BENCHES, LIKE THESE CURRENTLY FOUND ON THE TERRACES, THAT FEATURE A CHINESE-RAILING MOTIF SIMILAR TO THOSE ON MONTICELLO'S ROOF.

Abbé Corrêa's Room

DURING HIS RETIREMENT YEARS at Monticello, Jefferson received visitors so frequently that his granddaughter Ellen Coolidge commented that "almost every day for at least eight months of the year, brought its contingent of guests." Two rooms on the north side of the house were guest rooms, named for their most frequent occupants. The North Square Room was called "Abbé Corrêa's Room" after José Corrêa da Serra, a Portuguese naturalist who later became Portugal's minister plenipotentiary to the United States. Corrêa visited seven times in as many years on trips he called "pilgrimages," and described his hosts at Monticello as "the family I am most attached to in all America."

JOSÉ CORRÊA DA SERRA

Corrêa, like Jefferson, was a man of many intellectual pursuits. He earned a law degree, was ordained into the Roman Catholic Church, studied botany and geology, and helped found the Royal Academy of Sciences of Lisbon. Corrêa and Jefferson met at Monticello in 1813, and grew so close that in 1816 Jefferson invited Corrêa to live in his house permanently, the only nonfamily member ever extended such an offer.

1 ALCOVE BED WITH BLUE DAMASK CURTAINS AND COUNTERPANE, REPRESENTATIVE OF FABRIC JEFFERSON BOUGHT IN FRANCE IN THE 1780S

2 REPRODUCTION WALNUT PRESS

3 PORTRAIT OF CORRÊA BY REMBRANDT PEALE, CIRCA 1812–1813

4 CHIPPENDALE-STYLE CHEST ON STAND

5 LOUIS XVI ARMCHAIRS REPRESENTATIVE OF FURNITURE JEFFERSON BOUGHT IN FRANCE

a comfortable room . . . for retirement when you chose it, and a sociable family, full of affection & respect for you, when tired of being alone." —Thomas Jefferson

STUDY OF PLANTS

Corrêa, who enjoyed botanical "rambles" at Monticello, shared Jefferson's passion for plants. This *Clarkia pulchella,* or Pinkfairies, was discovered by Meriwether Lewis in Idaho during the Jefferson-supported expedition of 1804–1806 and named for his expedition partner, William Clark.

BOTANICAL MICRO-SCOPE FOR INSPECTING PLANT SPECIMENS

Madison's Room

JAMES AND DOLLEY MADISON were frequent guests at Monticello, visiting so often that one of the bedrooms became known as "Madison's Room." It has one of the two full-size closets in the house, shaped like a triangle so it aligns with the room's octagonal shape. The trellis motif on the wallpaper is patterned after a shadow of the original design. Jefferson ordered different wallpaper for other rooms in the house.

MONTICELLO LOOKING
TOWARD CHARLOTTESVILLE
(TOP) AND WEST FRONT
(BELOW), JANE BRADDICK
PETICOLAS, 1825

REPRODUCTION OF
TRELLIS-PATTERNED
WALLPAPER
FROM FRANCE

ALCOVE BED
WITH CLOSET
OVERHEAD

" . . . there is no sounder judgment than his." —Thomas Jefferson

JAMES MADISON

James Madison and Thomas Jefferson likely first met in 1776 while serving together as members of Virginia's House of Delegates. They crossed paths again in 1779, when Jefferson was governor and Madison one of his advisers. As a close friend and political ally, Jefferson helped Madison win election as the fourth president of the United States. Madison later succeeded Jefferson again, this time as rector of the University of Virginia after Jefferson's death.

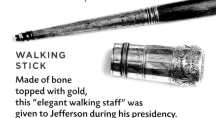

WALKING STICK

Made of bone topped with gold, this "elegant walking staff" was given to Jefferson during his presidency. He bequeathed it to Madison, who left it to Jefferson's grandson.

1,200+

LETTERS

were exchanged between Jefferson and Madison during nearly 50 years of friendship.

DOLLEY MADISON

Mrs. Madison sometimes served as Jefferson's hostess during his first presidential term, 1801–1805. He'd been a widower since his wife's death in 1782.

Stairs and Passages

RATHER THAN PLACING a grand stairway at the center of his house, Jefferson installed a modest staircase in each wing. He designed them to be narrow and steep to save "space that would make a good room in every story." He also built the hallways, called passages, to be flexible spaces. Besides providing access, the north passages served as storage areas, workrooms, and occasional sleeping quarters. Two passages in the basement led from rooms in the wings to the center of the house. The passages served as conduits for ventilation, and allowed enslaved servants to move efficiently while staying out of sight as much as possible.

✳ THE PEOPLE

Burwell Colbert

A grandson of Elizabeth (Betty) Hemings, Burwell Colbert began working in the nailmaking shop on Mulberry Row at age ten and later was trained as a painter and glazier. In Jefferson's retirement, Colbert became his personal servant and butler, managing enslaved housemaids, waiters, and porters. Jefferson paid him an annual gratuity of 20 dollars. Colbert was granted his freedom in Jefferson's will.

BELL SYSTEM

When Jefferson and his family wanted to summon an enslaved servant, they rang a system of bells attached to springs, like this one, found under the south stairway.

BURWELL COLBERT AS DEPICTED BY GAIL MCINTOSH, 2010

NORTH STAIRWAY

24

INCHES WIDE
was Jefferson's design
for the narrow stair-
cases, inspired by the
private staircases to
bedrooms in the "new
and good" houses
he saw in France.

*" I went to my chamber, found there a fire, candle,
and a servant in waiting to receive my orders
for the morning, and in the morning was waked
by his return to build the fire."* —George Ticknor

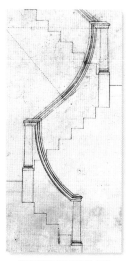

JEFFERSON RENDERED THIS
DRAWING OF THE MAIN
STAIRCASE FOR MONTICELLO I
AROUND 1771.

EFFICIENT SPACES

Jefferson steered away from grandeur in Monticello II,
emphasizing a more efficient use of space and easier movement about the house. Because of the alignment of the passages and staircases, enslaved servants brought food directly
from the kitchen to the north cellar, where it was put into
dishes and then taken to the Dining Room. The revolving
serving door (at right) was used to deliver dessert dishes
as well as to take away dishes from the first course.

Aunt Marks' Room

JEFFERSON WAS FOND OF his youngest sister, Anne Scott Jefferson Marks, who came to live at Monticello in early 1812, following the death of her husband, Hastings Marks, the previous year. As an elderly widow with no children or means of support, she was dependent on her extended family to take care of her, an obligation Jefferson willingly accepted. Today the second floor North Octagonal Room is represented as "Aunt Marks' Room," using the name she was given by the children and grandchildren in the house. Aunt Marks was not shy about offering her opinion, prompting Jefferson's granddaughter Mary to complain "[Aunt Marks] would not let me drink my tea without her advice."

16
YEARS
Aunt Marks lived at Monticello with Jefferson or his family.

THIS WALNUT PRESS WITH MAHOG-
ANY SHELVES WAS LIKELY FASH-
IONED BY JOHN HEMMINGS IN THE
MULBERRY ROW JOINER'S SHOP,
USING NAILS FROM THE NAILERY.

THIS TYPE OF PITCHER
AND BASIN WAS USED
FOR WASHING ONE'S
HANDS AND FACE.

RESTORATION
This room has been restored to look as it did during Jefferson's retirement. Research into the original paint dictated the colors today: gray on the walls, with cream white and dark gray blue for the woodwork. Other details include a Rittenhouse stove and furniture attributed to the Monticello joinery.

Window Illusion

Many of the changes Jefferson incorporated into Monticello II were inspired by the architecture he saw in France. About one trend, he remarked "in Paris particularly all the new & good houses are of a single story." On the East Front, Jefferson placed second-floor windows directly above those on the first floor, making each pair appear to be a single window. When viewed from the outside, the design creates the illusion of a single tall story. Except for the Dome Room, rooms on the third floor are illuminated entirely by skylights.

RITTENHOUSE STOVE

This type of stove, named for the inventor David Rittenhouse, is a simplification of a design by Benjamin Franklin. It is believed to be original to Monticello.

THIS SMALL, PORTABLE MEDICINE CHEST WAS USED TO CARRY 18 GLASS BOTTLES.

A BOTTOM DRAWER OF THIS PHILADELPHIA HIGH CHEST, CIRCA 1755, HELD CHILDREN'S GAMES AND TOYS.

THE BEDSTEAD WITH CURTAIN RODS WAS MODELED AFTER JEFFERSON'S DESIGN FOR "AN ECONOMICAL CURTAIN BEDSTEAD."

MARTHA JEFFERSON RANDOLPH

This 1836 portrait was painted by the Philadelphia artist Thomas Sully.

Martha Jefferson Randolph's Room

KNOWN AS PATSY to family and friends, Martha Jefferson Randolph was the first child of Thomas Jefferson and his wife, Martha Wayles Skelton. Following her mother's death in 1782, the ten-year-old became her father's "constant companion" in his grief, establishing a lifelong closeness. Later in Washington, D.C., she sometimes acted as hostess at the President's House. She moved to Monticello with her family after her father's retirement, and took responsibility for educating her children and supervising the plantation's domestic activities. "She was graceful in figure and movement, an accomplished musician, well acquainted with several languages, well grounded in all the solid branches of a woman's education," her daughter Ellen recalled.

STORAGE BOX

Boxes like this offered fashionable storage for a lady's sewing and writing implements, as well as personal items. Martha's box is covered in red leather and has ormolu paw feet.

Nursery

JEFFERSON, A DEVOTED grandfather who paid special attention to the education and welfare of his family, designated a room to serve as a nursery—something that was uncommon at the time—as he planned the expansion of Monticello in the 1790s. Over the years, the Nursery was occupied by a number of Jefferson's young grandchildren, great-grandchildren, and their visiting cousins. Martha Jefferson Randolph and enslaved nurse Priscilla Hemmings oversaw the care of the children and the management of the Nursery, which was adjacent to Martha's bedroom. Jefferson's grandchildren were particularly fond of Priscilla. After Priscilla's death in 1830, Cornelia Jefferson Randolph wrote "there were a thousand little attentions she paid us, & some very troublesome to herself."

SEPTIMIA'S DOLLHOUSE

Septimia Anne Randolph, affectionately called "pet" or "Tim" by her family, was the seventh and last daughter born to Martha Jefferson Randolph and Thomas Mann Randolph. Later in life, she explained that her small walnut cabinet with a glass door originally served as a dollhouse for her "dolls, their furniture and their clothes, and many playthings." It was designed by Jefferson and built in Monticello's joinery by an enslaved carpenter, thought to be John Hemmings. In the nursery, Jefferson's granddaughters played with dolls (like the reproduction shown here), fashioning clothing from scraps of ribbon and fabric with the help of their mother, Martha, and family friend Dolley Madison.

THE CRADLE IS BASED ON A SKETCH AND MEASUREMENTS JEFFERSON MADE.

82

North Bedroom

LOCATED AT THE northeast corner of the third floor, the North Bedroom has been interpreted as a space where Jefferson's grandsons slept during his retirement years at Monticello. Visitors today are invited to open the chests, feel the mattresses, and explore other objects in the room, which are reproductions. Twin alcoves, bedding areas built to accommodate double beds, are examples of features Jefferson incorporated into his Virginia home as a result of French influence. Efficiency was a practical consideration, because Jefferson's daughter, her husband, and many of his grandchildren and great-grandchildren lived with him during his retirement years. Preserving the illusion that the house is one tall story, skylights in recessed alcoves provide sunlight and ventilation. Overlapping panes of glass keep rain from leaking in.

✳ THE PEOPLE

Grandsons

Thomas Jefferson's daughter Martha had five sons, most named after Jefferson's friends. The oldest, Thomas Jefferson Randolph, would later settle the family debt. Next in age were James Madison and Benjamin Franklin Randolph, who both attended the University of Virginia, and Meriwether Lewis Randolph who, like his namesake, moved west to Arkansas. Youngest was George Wythe Randolph, named for Virginia's first signatory of the Declaration of Independence, who served as secretary of war for the Confederacy. Jefferson's daughter Maria had one son, Francis Wayles Eppes, whom Jefferson helped raise after Maria's death.

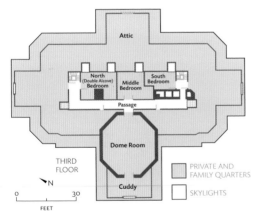

THIRD FLOOR

Attic

North (Double Alcove) Bedroom | Middle Bedroom | South Bedroom

Passage

Dome Room

Cuddy

PRIVATE AND FAMILY QUARTERS

SKYLIGHTS

0 — 30 FEET

N

NATURAL LIGHTING
Of the house's 13 skylights, four are over the third-floor bedrooms. Others include the Dome Room oculus, two large skylights over the Dining Room and Jefferson's bedchamber, and the remaining six over the two stairwells, two privies, and the steps to the roofs.

12

JEFFERSON GRANDCHILDREN

lived or spent time at Monticello during Jefferson's retirement.

7

JEFFERSON SIBLINGS

included 6 sisters and 1 brother. Only 2 sisters and his brother lived past age 30.

GEORGE WYTHE RANDOLPH

MERIWETHER LEWIS RANDOLPH

FRANCIS WAYLES EPPES

BENJAMIN FRANKLIN RANDOLPH

THOMAS JEFFERSON RANDOLPH

Dome Room

THE EXTERIOR OF the Dome Room, Monticello's iconic design element, was based on the Temple of Vesta in Rome as depicted by Palladio. An architectural conceit, the dome was primarily meant to be seen from the outside. Looking up at the ceiling inside, visitors will notice a pattern of rectangles shrinking in size and the oculus at the center of the dome. Sometimes called the "skyroom," the Dome Room was at times used for guests, as temporary living quarters for Jefferson's grandson and his wife, and for storage. Washington socialite Margaret Bayard Smith, an author and family friend, noted, "It is a noble & beautiful apartment . . . not furnished, & being in the attic story, is not used.—which I thought a great pity, as it might be made the most beautiful room in the house."

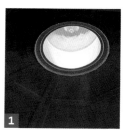

1

THE CIRCULAR OPENING IS CALLED AN OCULUS, LATIN FOR "EYE."

2

FOUR OUTWARD-FACING FULL WINDOWS PROVIDE LIGHT AND DRAMATIC VIEWS.

HALF-MIRRORED WINDOWS

Two such windows conceal the main block of the house.

3

THE CEILING CORNICE IS MOD-ELED AFTER THE COURTYARD WALL OF THE TEMPLE OF NERVA TRAJAN.

4

THE BASE MOLDING IS SCALED TO THE HEIGHT OF MONTICELLO, RATHER THAN OF THE ROOM.

49

POUNDS
The weight of the glass skylight in the oculus

DETAIL FROM JEFFERSON'S NOTES ON THE CURVE OF THE DOME, 1796

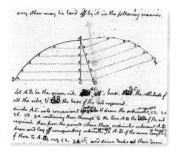

✳ THE PEOPLE

Thomas Jefferson Randolph

The only known residents of the Dome Room during Jefferson's lifetime were his grandson Thomas Jefferson "Jeff" Randolph and wife Jane Hollins Nicholas, who lived there briefly. Jeff was born at Monticello in 1792. At age 15 he was sent to Philadelphia to study at the University of Pennsylvania. He returned to Monticello four years later. In 1815, he and Jane were married, and lived together in the Dome Room. Two years later, they moved to Tufton, one of Monticello's quarter farms (see p. 108). Jeff took over management of Jefferson's farms. Later in his life, Jeff was able to repay the debts left by his grandfather's estate.

The Cuddy

PRIVATE SPACES FOR READING, drawing, and studying were often hard to find in a house crowded with Jefferson's family and frequent guests. In 1823, when the Doric columns of the West Portico were completed and Jefferson had the workbench removed from the attic space above the portico, two of his adult granddaughters seized their opportunity to create a hideaway. Virginia Jefferson Randolph and her older sister, Cornelia, used boxes as steps to get from the Dome Room down into the attic space they called their cuddy. To complete the space, they added what Virginia described as "a sopha to lounge upon, though alas! without cushions, a high & low chair & two small tables, one for my writing desk, the other for my books . . ."

"CUDDY" WINDOW ABOVE THE WEST PORTICO

VIRGINIA RANDOLPH TRIST (AT LEFT, WITH SISTER ELLEN RANDOLPH COOLIDGE) WROTE HER FIANCÉ THAT SHE AND HER SISTER CORNELIA HAD TURNED AN UNUSED ATTIC INTO A "FAIRY PALACE."

1

SURVIVING SILKWORM in his granddaughters' failing silkworm colony caused Jefferson to tease them that they could not marry until it had spun enough silk for wedding dresses.

SECRET ENTRANCE Before she married, Virginia described "the *nice little cuddy* that has become my haunt" to her future husband, Nicholas Trist, telling him how the Dome Room opened into this little hideaway, rather than to an expansive view.

" *I have taken possession with the dirt daubers, wasps & humble bees; and do not intend to give it up to any thing but the formidable rats which have not yet found out this* fairy palace." —Virginia Jefferson Randolph (Trist)

DRAWING OF A TABLE AND CHAIR
AT POPLAR FOREST BY CORNELIA
JEFFERSON RANDOLPH

YOUNG ARTISTS

Jefferson taught his granddaughter Cornelia to sketch and paint. This palette and paint set are hers. Jefferson encouraged creativity in the young family members.

SOUTH PAVILION

CONSTRUCTION OF MONTICELLO began in 1770 with a two-story brick structure that Jefferson called the outchamber, now known as the South Pavilion, the oldest brick structure on the landscape and Jefferson's first home at Monticello. A simple living space on the upper floor with a kitchen below, each measuring just 18 feet by 18 feet, it became a family residence after Jefferson's marriage to Martha Wayles Skelton in January 1772. From here Jefferson planned and began constructing the original eight-room Monticello I, where he and Martha lived until her death in 1782. She would never experience today's Monticello that Jefferson enlarged and redesigned after his return from France.

✳ THE HOUSE

MARTHA JEFFERSON AT MONTICELLO

The one-room living space that initially sheltered Jefferson alone in 1770 welcomed his wife, Martha, in 1772. She had recently lost her first husband, Bathurst Skelton, and young son, John. Later that year she gave birth in this room to the eldest Jefferson daughter, Martha, beginning her second family. From this space Martha would have begun her duties of overseeing Monticello's domestic operations. Described by one family member as a "graceful, ladylike, and accomplished woman," she was also known for her "greatest fund of good nature." Beloved by Jefferson, Martha would bear five more children before her death in 1782.

THE SOUTH PAVILION

" I have lately removed to the mountain . . . I have here but one room, which, like the cobler's, serves me for parlour for kitchen and hall." —Thomas Jefferson

THE WHITE RAILS IN THIS 2014 IMAGE WERE RETURNED TO THE ORIGINAL DESIGN AND GREEN COLOR IN 2017.

1 THIS RANDOLPH FAMILY THREE-SIDED CRIB MAY HAVE HELD THE JEFFERSONS' FIRST NEWBORN ADJACENT TO THE BEDSTEAD

2 A SECRETARY BOOKCASE WAS THE HUB FOR DIRECTING THE BUSINESS OF THE HOUSEHOLD AND FARM.

3 THE REPRODUCTION BEDSTEAD FEATURES FASHIONABLE PRINTED COTTON HANGINGS LIKE THOSE ORDERED FROM WILLIAMSBURG UPHOLSTERER JOSEPH KIDD.

4 SIDE CHAIRS, AS WELL AS A LIBRARY CHAIR AND SLIP-COVERED EASY CHAIR, PROVIDED SEATING

5 A GRACEFUL DINING TABLE HELD PEWTER, CREAMWARE, AND BRASS CANDLESTICKS.

North Pavilion

MIRRORING THE SOUTH PAVILION, the construction of the North Pavilion completed Jefferson's scheme for organizing domestic functions. The upper floor, like that of the South Pavilion, was used by members of Jefferson's family: Son-in-law Thomas Mann Randolph used it as a study, while granddaughter Virginia Randolph and her husband Nicholas Trist lived there after their marriage in 1824. The cellar may first have been a storehouse for wood or supplies, and then a place for bathing until about 1818. Later it was used as a washhouse for laundry. Ice and snow from the icehouse quelled a fire here in 1819.

KINDRED SPIRIT

Often using the pavilion study (above), Thomas Mann Randolph, husband of Jefferson's daughter Martha, shared numerous interests with his father-in-law. A respected botanist, he experimented with scientific agriculture and, in the course of his political career, served as governor of Virginia, congressman, state delegate, and state senator.

THOMAS MANN RANDOLPH (1768–1828) WAS MARRIED TO MARTHA JEFFERSON RANDOLPH.

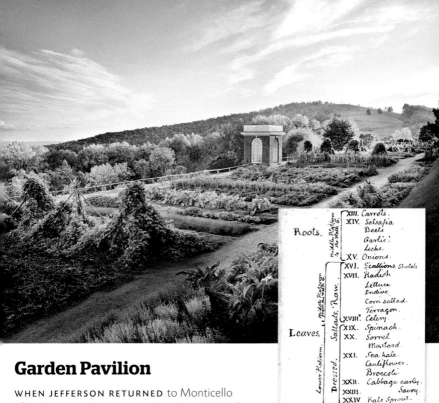

Garden Pavilion

WHEN JEFFERSON RETURNED to Monticello after his second term as president, he gladly left politics behind, preferring "to indulge the evening of my life with what have been the passions of every portion of it, books, science, my farms, my family and friends. to these every hour of the day is now devoted." Among his favorite passions was enjoying the gardens and orchards southeast of the house, where he located a pavilion in his garden. Constructed in 1812 and rebuilt in 1984, the building is a cube with sides measuring 12 feet seven inches each.

GARDEN BOOK
Jefferson kept a meticulous and detailed daily record of his plantings, as well as of rainfall and weather.

VEGETABLE GARDEN
At its peak in 1812, the 1,000-foot-long terraced garden was divided into 24 plots. As his notes show, Jefferson organized the garden by the part of the plant to be harvested: "fruits" (tomatoes), "roots" (beets), or "leaves" (lettuce).

North and South Wings

JEFFERSON DESIGNED THE "wings" under the L-shaped terraces to hold the facilities required for domestic operations. This concept was borrowed from Renaissance architect Andrea Palladio, who used wings extending from the main house around a courtyard to house service areas. Jefferson modified this idea by facing the entrances outward and tucking them into the landscape to preserve uninterrupted views. The terraces covering the wings may have been inspired by 18th-century enlightened Scottish agriculturalist Lord Kames, who suggested walkways above the terrain to "elevate the mind." Jefferson built Monticello's walkways closer to the ground than those seen in England or Europe, creating a unique sense of connection with nature.

✳ THE HOUSE

In Each Wing

The South Wing connects the South Pavilion to the all-weather passage that runs under the main house and contained the post-1809 kitchen, cook's room (where the head cook lived), smokehouse, two living quarters for enslaved workers (one room occupied by Sally Hemings and her children), and the dairy. The icehouse, tack room, and bays for horses and carriages were located in the North Wing, which connects the passage under the house to the North Pavilion (constructed in 1809, more than 30 years after the South Pavilion). Each side had an indoor, nonflushable toilet called a privy.

ARCHAEOLOGICAL EXCAVATIONS UNDER THE SOUTH PAVILION RELOCATED THE BRICK FLOOR OF THE ORIGINAL MONTICELLO KITCHEN, CALLED GRANGER/HEMINGS KITCHEN, AND THE REMAINS OF A EUROPEAN-INSPIRED STEW STOVE, WHICH ALLOWED FOR MORE PRECISION THAN DID AN OPEN-FIRE HEARTH.

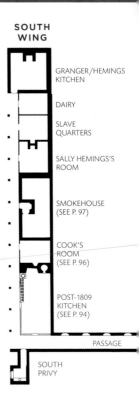

SOUTH WING

GRANGER/HEMINGS KITCHEN

DAIRY

SLAVE QUARTERS

SALLY HEMINGS'S ROOM

SMOKEHOUSE (SEE P. 97)

COOK'S ROOM (SEE P. 96)

POST-1809 KITCHEN (SEE P. 94)

PASSAGE

SOUTH PRIVY

> *The house has been fifty six years building and is still unfinished.*" —Ellen W. Randolph Coolidge

38

YEARS
Design of the wings began ca. 1770; construction was completed in 1809.

THE KITCHEN IS ON THE RIGHT IN THIS VIEW OF THE PROTECTED SOUTH WING.

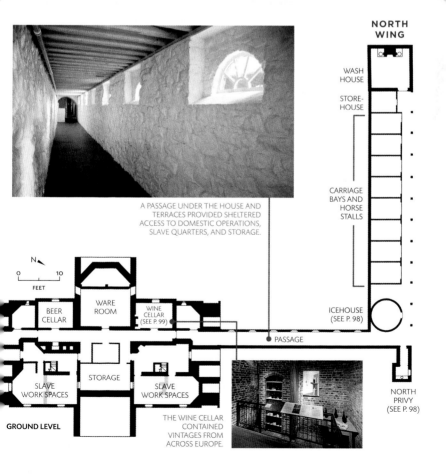

A PASSAGE UNDER THE HOUSE AND TERRACES PROVIDED SHELTERED ACCESS TO DOMESTIC OPERATIONS, SLAVE QUARTERS, AND STORAGE.

NORTH WING

WASH HOUSE

STORE-HOUSE

CARRIAGE BAYS AND HORSE STALLS

ICEHOUSE (SEE P. 98)

N

0   10
FEET

BEER CELLAR

WARE ROOM

WINE CELLAR (SEE P. 99)

PASSAGE

STORAGE

SLAVE WORK SPACES

SLAVE WORK SPACES

NORTH PRIVY (SEE P. 98)

GROUND LEVEL

THE WINE CELLAR CONTAINED VINTAGES FROM ACROSS EUROPE.

Kitchen

BY 1809, WHEN JEFFERSON RETURNED to Monticello from Washington, the Kitchen had moved to its new location in the just completed South Wing. Not only was it a much larger space for food preparation than the old Kitchen in the basement of the South Pavilion, and closer to the house, it was also among the best equipped kitchens in America. One piece of equipment rarely seen outside Europe was the stew stove, which had cast-iron openings that were individually heated by hot coals, allowing for temperature regulation like a modern stove. Cooks prepared bread in the bake oven and used some 60 copper pots and pans and pieces of specialized cookware shipped by Jefferson from France in 1790.

BRICKS WERE LAID ON THEIR SIDE TO BUILD THE ORIGINAL FLOOR.

THIS BUILT-IN "SET KETTLE" PROVIDED CONSTANT HOT WATER.

THIS SPIT JACK W⬛ USED TO ROTATE M⬛ AND POULTRY ROA⬛ ING OVER THE FIR⬛

I have lived temperately, eating little animal food . . . vegetables . . . constitute my principal diet."

—Thomas Jefferson

JEFFERSON PURCHASED
COPPER KITCHENWARE
IN FRANCE.

Inventory of Kitchen utincils

19 Copper Stew pans — 19 Covers
6 Small Sauce pans
3 Copper Baking Moulds
2 Small preserving pans
2 Large ———— Ditto
2 Copper Fish kettles
2 Copper Brazing pans
2 Round Large ———— Ditto
2 Iron Stew pans
2 Large Boiling kettles lind inside
1 Large Brass ———— Ditto
12 pewter water Dishes
12 ———— plates
3 Tin Coffie pots
8 Tin Dish Covers
2 frying pans of Iron & one of Copper
4 Round Baking Copper Sheets lind
4 Square Copper Ditto unlind
1 Copper Boiler
1 Copper tea kettle / 1 Iron Ditto

KITCHEN INVENTORY

James Hemings recorded this two-page list of kitchen utensils in 1796 before he left Monticello.

✳ THE PEOPLE

Edith Fossett, Head Cook

Edith Hern was born in 1787 to David and Isabel Hern, who were both slaves at Monticello. When Edith was 15 years old, Jefferson brought her and her sister-in-law Frances Hern to Washington to learn French cookery at the President's House (now the White House). They studied under Honoré Julien, a French chef hired by Jefferson. During this time, Edith was separated from her husband Joseph Fossett, an enslaved blacksmith, with only occasional visits. In 1809, at the end of Jefferson's second term as president, she returned to Monticello and became head cook, one of the most responsible positions in the household. Assisted by enslaved girls, she roasted meat, cooked vegetables from the garden, and prepared churned ice cream. When Daniel Webster described Monticello's cuisine as being in "half Virginian, half French style," he was referring to Edith Fossett's cooking.

Cook's Room

THE COOK'S ROOM, adjacent to the Kitchen in the South Wing, was occupied by Monticello's head cook. It was first used as living quarters by Peter Hemings, followed likely by Edith Fossett and her family in 1809. While the exact contents of the room are unknown, the items seen below are based on the study of Jefferson's records, including rations, historical documents, and artifacts of the period. The Fossett family— Edith, Joseph, and some of their eight children—shared 140 square feet of space. In the evenings, they used the room in a variety of ways such as cooking, sewing, and even spelling, according to their son Peter.

THIS CHINESE EXPORT PLATE HAS A "PEONY" PATTERN.

ITEMS SUCH AS A BEDSTEAD, BED, COVERLET, CHAIR, AND PINE TABLE REFLECT THE STATUS AND MEANS OF THE FOSSETT FAMILY.

ACTIVITIES SUCH AS SEWING AND MENDING OCCUPIED THE FOSSETTS' EVENINGS.

EVEN THOUGH EDITH FOSSETT WAS HEAD COOK, HER FAMILY PREPARED THEIR OWN MEALS. THEIR FOOD RATIONS ARE LISTED IN THE FARM BOOK.

FOSSETT FAMILY

As foreman of the blacksmith shop and head cook, Joseph and Edith Fossett held important positions at Monticello. Although Jefferson's will granted Joseph his freedom, Edith and seven of their children, including Peter (left), remained enslaved and were sold at auction. Joseph worked tirelessly to reunite his family, and by the 1850s, Joseph, Edith, and most of their children lived free in Ohio.

23

YEARS

after Peter Fossett (1815–1901) was sold into bondage to a Charlottesville owner, he finally joined his family in Ohio, in 1850.

Smokehouse

MONTICELLO'S SMOKEHOUSE moved in 1802 from Mulberry Row to a room near the center of the South Wing. Meat was butchered and preserved through salting and smoking during winter, when the cold minimized spoilage. In addition to traditional methods of pest control, like wrapping meat in linen bags or covering it with ash, Jefferson suggested installing a barrier shelf around the upper edge of the room to deter rodents. (No evidence of the barrier exists.) The most desirable meats, like ham and bacon, were served to the family, while lower quality parts were given to enslaved workers.

THE JOINTS OF PORK.

1 Spare-rib
2 Hand
3 Belly or spring
4 Fore-loin
5 Hind-loin
6 Leg

PRESERVING MEAT

The smokehouse (above) included a fireplace that could be stoked from the outside while the meat remained locked away behind it. Once the main cuts of meat were butchered from a cow or pig (left), enslaved servants Ursula Granger and John (surname unknown) cut the meat into smaller pieces, such as bacon; covered it in salt; and hung it by a low-burning fire to cure (below).

1½
DAYS PER POUND
is the time it takes to cure a Virginia-style ham.

Virginia Ham

A cook from Thomas Jefferson's day would probably not have recognized modern deli-style ham as ham at all. Until the 20th century, all ham was created using traditional preservation methods: by salt curing (and sometimes smoking) pork rather than by cooking it with heat. The result was essentially what we call country ham—mostly dry, reddish, salty meat. Cooked meat at Monticello would have spoiled quickly without refrigeration, whereas cured meat, such as the slices of ham here, lasted as long as needed.

Icehouse

THOMAS JEFFERSON NEEDED ICE for food preservation. During the summer of 1792 in Philadelphia, he paid 1 shilling a day for an ice delivery subscription. Nine years later, he had an icehouse built at the President's House in Washington. During the winter of 1802–1803, he instructed overseer Gabriel Lilly to build a round structure 16 feet in diameter and 16 feet deep in the coldest location at Monticello, under the North Terrace. The icehouse was used primarily to store fresh meat and butter, and to chill wine. Packed tightly and insulated with wood chips or straw, the ice sometimes lasted through summer.

HARVESTING ICE

Stockpiling ice was a critical winter task. Without ice, fresh meat and dairy products would spoil quickly during the hot Virginia summers. Filling the icehouse was labor intensive and costly. The first year it was used, 62 wagonsful of ice had to be hauled from the Rivanna River to the top of Monticello Mountain. The cost of hiring and feeding drivers was $70, the equivalent of at least $1,300 today.

1

INCH THICK
was the depth of river ice harvested for the icehouse.

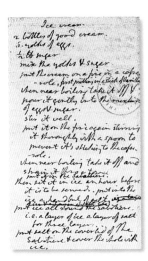

ICE CREAM RECIPE

Jefferson's ice cream recipe, likely from his French butler Adrien Petit, was the first to be recorded by an American. One of ten recipes in existence handwritten by Jefferson, it calls for "2. bottles of good cream., 6. yolks of eggs, 1/2 lb. sugar."

❋ THE HOUSE

North Privy

Although it was unusual for houses in the United States at the start of the 19th century to have toilet facilities inside them, Monticello had three: one near Jefferson's chamber and two on the south side of the house. Two more privies were located nearby at the ends of the north and south passages. These nonflushing privies were attached to shafts that provided ventilation. Slaves were paid a gratuity to clean them. A necessary was also located on Mulberry Row.

Wine Cellar

IN AN 1815 LETTER, Jefferson wrote that "wine from long habit has become an indispensable for my health . . ." As one of the most knowledgeable experts in the country, he served as wine adviser to Presidents Washington, Madison, and Monroe. His cellar was filled with wines from France, Portugal, Spain, Hungary, Germany, and Italy, reflecting tastes he acquired during his years in France. Jefferson sometimes imported several hundred bottles a year. He preferred bottles to casks, because casks could be adulterated by wine merchants or by crewmen on board a vessel during shipment.

382

BOTTLES OF WINE

were received by Jefferson for his cellar, as noted in a record from 1820.

WINE DUMBWAITERS

Hidden dumbwaiters on either side of the fireplace in the Dining Room delivered bottles of wine from the cellar directly below, while causing minimal disturbance to diners. Enslaved butler Burwell Colbert would load two bottles at a time onto each trolley and deliver it upstairs via a pulley system. In the Dining Room, serving wine was as simple as opening the side door and retrieving the waiting bottles.

The Plantation

Jefferson envisioned Monticello's
gardens, grounds, orchards, and
vineyards as living laboratories.

A Working Plantation

MONTICELLO WAS MORE THAN Thomas Jefferson's home. It was also a working enterprise, one of several plantations that supported him and his family. On these lands Jefferson experimented with revolutionary ideas about farming and gardening, using the labor of people he held in slavery. At any given time, 130 enslaved men, women, and children worked at Monticello in dozens of occupations from field laborers, house servants, artisans, sawyers, and charcoal burners to gardeners and blacksmiths. He incorporated Enlightenment thinking in the management of his slave workforce and used his gardens, orchard, and vineyard as testing grounds to determine which flowers, trees, vegetables, and fruits would grow most successfully on his land. Despite Jefferson's experimentation, including with light industries and the labor of his slaves, the plantation was unprofitable and he was often in debt.

"Agriculture . . . is our wisest pursuit, because it will in the end contribute most to real wealth, good morals & happiness."

—Thomas Jefferson

DETAIL OF BENJAMIN H. LATROBE'S 1798 WATERCOLOR OF A VIRGINIA FARM, "AN OVERSEER DOING HIS DUTY"

PLANTING TIME

Like workers at other plantations in Virginia (left), enslaved laborers at Monticello worked from dawn to dark, six days a week. While some tended crops and livestock, others played essential roles on Mulberry Row and in the house as carpenters, black-smiths, weavers, cooks, butlers, maids, and nursemaids.

130+

SLAVES

worked at Monticello at any given time.

Slavery at Monticello

THOMAS JEFFERSON HELPED TO CREATE a new nation based on individual freedom and self-government. His words in the Declaration of Independence expressed the aspirations of the new nation. African Americans, however, were excluded from the promise of "Life, Liberty, and the pursuit of Happiness" that was asserted in the declaration. Jefferson called slavery an "abominable crime," yet he was a lifelong slaveholder. Fearful of dividing the fragile new nation, he and other founders who opposed slavery did not insist on abolishing it.

More than 600 slaves worked at Monticello and Jefferson's other properties during his lifetime. He initially acquired most of his slaves through inheritance from his father and father-in-law. The majority of slaves at Monticello were farm laborers who lived near the fields they worked. Enslaved house servants and artisans lived in log dwellings on the mountaintop along Mulberry Row or in rooms beneath the South Terrace of the main house.

ISAAC GRANGER JEFFERSON

Born in 1775, Isaac Granger Jefferson, the youngest son of enslaved overseer George Granger, Sr., learned blacksmithing from his brother George and tinsmithing in Philadelphia. At Monticello he was a tinsmith, blacksmith, and in 1796 was the most productive nailer. After gaining his freedom around age 50, Isaac was known by the surname Jefferson. In the 1840s, while living in Petersburg, Virginia, he shared his memories of Monticello with the Reverend Charles Campbell, who described him as "tall of strong frame . . . sensible, intelligent, pleasant."

20+

SLAVES

tried to escape from Monticello between 1769 and 1819. Those who sought freedom rarely succeeded.

RUN away from the subscriber in *Albemarle*, a Mulatto slave called *Sandy*, about 35 years of age, his stature is rather low, inclining to corpulence, and his complexion light; he is a shoemaker by trade, in which he uses his left hand principally, can do coarse carpenters work, and is something of a horse jockey; he is greatly addicted to drink, and when drunk is insolent and disorderly, in his conversation he swears much, and in his behaviour is artful and knavish. He took with him a white horse, much scarred with traces, of which it is expected he will endeavour to dispose; he also carried his shoemakers tools, and will probably endeavour to get employment that way. Whoever conveys the said slave to me, in *Albemarle*, shall have 40 s. reward, if taken up within the county, 4 l. if elsewhere within the colony, and 10 l. if in any other colony, from
THOMAS JEFFERSON.

607

ENSLAVED PEOPLE
were owned by Jefferson in
his lifetime.

TIN CUP, PROBA-
BLY MADE BY
ISAAC GRANGER
JEFFERSON,
FOUND DURING
EXCAVATIONS OF
MULBERRY ROW

> " *The whole commerce between master
> and slave is a perpetual exercise of
> the most boisterous passions, the
> most unremitting despotism on the
> one part, and degrading submissions
> on the other. Our children see this,
> and learn to imitate it; for man is
> an imitative animal.*" —Thomas Jefferson

Treatment of Slaves

"my first wish is that the labourers may
be well treated," Jefferson wrote in
1792, "the second that they may enable
me to have that treatment continued
by making as much as will admit it." He
attempted to balance the humane
treatment of slaves with the need for
hard work and the income it provided.
Rather than use force to compel his
slaves to work, he sometimes offered
financial incentives—gratuities (tips),
special privileges, or percentages of
workshop profits—to those who maxi-
mized efficiency and output.

A former Monticello slave, Peter
Fossett (1815–1901), recalled that
"slaves were seldom punished,
except for stealing and fighting." Most
known incidents of brutality came from
overseers and stewards. To support
his more "rational and humane plan"
of treatment, Jefferson sought overseers who embraced his approach.
He stipulated that the whip "must
not be resorted to but in extremities,"
but his instructions were often ignored
during his long absences. In the
Mulberry Row nailery, for example,
the "small ones" could be whipped for
"truancy." In the fields, enslaved men
or women could be flogged for arriving
late or weeding too slowly.

"ROLL OF THE
NEGROES TAKEN IN
1783," FARM BOOK

[Handwritten list from the Farm Book: "Roll of the negroes taken in..." — names and ages of enslaved people.]

Enslaved People
Generations of extended families

THE MONTICELLO PLANTATION was a complex community dependent on the labor of many people—especially its enslaved field laborers, artisans, and domestic workers. Enslaved people worked from sunrise to sunset six days a week, with Sundays and a few holidays off. In their limited free time, slaves at Monticello created strong family bonds and meaningful social, cultural, and spiritual lives independent of Jefferson. They held

THE HEMINGS FAMILY
More than 70 members of the Hemings family lived in slavery at Monticello over five generations. Elizabeth Hemings (1735–1807) and her children arrived at Monticello around 1774 as part of Thomas Jefferson's inheritance from his father-in-law, John Wayles, who was likely the father of six of the children. Hemings family members eventually occupied the most important positions in Monticello's labor force. They helped build the Monticello house, ran the household, made furniture, cooked Jefferson's meals, cared for his children and grandchildren, attended him in his final moments, and dug his grave.

Elk-hill cont

+ Betty Hemings.
  Nancy. 1761.
  Thenia. 1767.
  Critta. 1769.
  Peter. Aug. 1770.
  Sally. 1773.
  Daniel. 1772.

DOCUMENT NAMING SIX CHILDREN OF ELIZABETH "BETTY" HEMINGS, WITH BIRTH DATES

BUYING POWER
Monticello slaves received a weekly ration (partially shown at left), which included a peck of cornmeal, three to four fish, and a half pound of fatback pork or pickled beef per adult. To supplement it, slaves worked at night and on Sundays, growing food and raising chickens to sell to the Jefferson family and in Charlottesville's Sunday market for cash payments. Some slaves also earned tips and cash. Money went to buy clothing and household goods.

This indenture witnesseth that I Thomas Jefferson of the county of Albemarle have manumitted and made free Robert Hemings, son of Betty Hemings: so that in future he shall be free & of free condition, with all his goods & chat and shall be discharged of all obligation of bondage or servitu whatsoever: and that neither myself my hei

10

MONTICELLO SLAVES
gained their freedom in Jefferson's lifetime and in h will. All ten were members c the extended Hemings fam

DEED OF MANUMISSION
GRANTING FREEDOM TO
ROBERT HEMINGS, 1794

> *"We were free from the dread of having to be slaves all our lives long."* —Madison Hemings

worship services, played games and musical instruments, and a few learned to read and write. Several extended families lived in slavery at Monticello for three or more generations. Among them were the Hemingses, the Gillettes, the Grangers, the Herns, and the Hubbards. ✤

THIS PHARMACEUTICAL JAR MAY HAVE COME FROM PARIS WITH SALLY HEMINGS.

✳ THE PEOPLE

Sally Hemings

Sally Hemings (1773–1835) came to Monticello as a baby with her mother and siblings around 1774. At 14, she accompanied Jefferson's daughter Mary (later Maria) to Paris as a lady's maid. Her son Madison recalled that her later duties at Monticello were to "take care of [Jefferson's] chamber and wardrobe, look after us children and do . . . light work." Since 1802, oral and published histories and other documents have identified Jefferson as the father of Sally Hemings's children. A 1998 DNA study genetically linked one of Hemings's male descendants with the Jefferson male line, lending scientific evidence. Oldest son Beverly and his sister Harriet were allowed to leave Monticello in 1822; younger sons Madison and Eston were freed in Jefferson's will. After Jefferson died, Sally lived out her life in unofficial freedom in Charlottesville.

BEVERLY JEFFERSON (SON OF ESTON HEMINGS AND JULIA ISAACS JEFFERSON AND GRANDSON OF SALLY HEMINGS) WITH THREE OF HIS FIVE SONS

5

GENERATIONS
of the Hemings family were slaves at Monticello.

DESCENDANTS

Since 1993, Monticello's "Getting Word" oral history project has strived to preserve the family histories of African Americans who lived at Monticello. Archival research and more than 100 interviews provided the crucial information needed to keep the contributions of the enslaved community from fading into history. Visit *slavery.monticello.org/getting-word*, where you can read firsthand stories, meet descendants who discovered their connection to Monticello, and follow the paths of families as they moved away from Virginia.

COL. JOHN WAYLES JEFFERSON, THE OLDEST SON OF ESTON HEMINGS, WAS A UNION ARMY OFFICER, HOTELKEEPER, AND COTTON MERCHANT.

ELLEN HEMINGS ROBERTS, THE YOUNGEST CHILD OF MADISON HEMINGS (SON OF SALLY HEMINGS) MOVED FROM OHIO TO CALIFORNIA IN 1887.

Farming

JEFFERSON RAISED COMMERCIAL CROPS on his plantation's three "quarter farms" adjacent to the Monticello "home farm": Tufton to the east, and Lego and Shadwell to the north across the Rivanna River. Enslaved men and women cultivated the crops; tended the livestock; and repaired fences, buildings, and machinery under the eye of an overseer at each farm. Until the 1790s, tobacco was Jefferson's main cash crop, just as it had been for his father. But after his retirement as secretary of state in 1794, Jefferson switched to wheat and rye. The grains were processed into flour at two state-of-the-art mills Jefferson owned at Shadwell. They were then packed in barrels made by Jefferson's coopers and shipped down the Rivanna River to Richmond. Often hobbled by debt and later by depressed markets, his farms seldom made a profit.

MILL AT SHADWELL

Driven by waterwheels, Jefferson's Mill at Shadwell (photographed in the 1870s) was the larger of two built on the Rivanna River. Both of the mills ground wheat into flour for sale at market and for use at Monticello.

5,000

ACRES OF PROPERTY

in Albemarle County were owned by Jefferson.

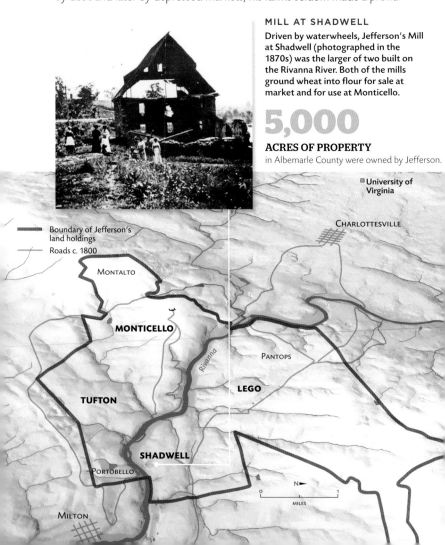

Boundary of Jefferson's land holdings
Roads c. 1800

University of Virginia
CHARLOTTESVILLE
MONTALTO
MONTICELLO
PANTOPS
Rivanna
LEGO
TUFTON
SHADWELL
PORTOBELLO
MILTON

N►
0 MILES 1

> *"cultivators of the earth are the most valuable citizens."*
> —Thomas Jefferson

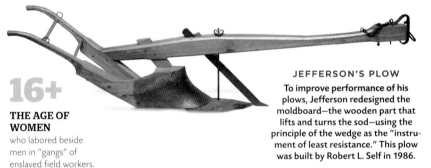

```
4. { Clover
5. fields of 64 a each
1. wheat                    800
2. Patches                       40
3. Rye                      800
4. Clover }
5. Clover }
6. fields of 53⅓ a each
1. wheat                  666⅔
2. Patches                      66
3. Rye or Oats            666⅔
4. Clover }
5. Clover }
6. Cowpea
```

FROM TOBACCO TO WHEAT

Calling himself "the most industrious & ardent farmer" in Virginia, Jefferson sought to bring new ideas and technologies to American agriculture. Switching from tobacco to wheat was part of this effort, driven by his belief that tobacco was "productive of infinite wretchedness," due to its damaging effects on the soil and the exhausting labor required for its cultivation. Inspired by English and American reformers, Jefferson in 1794 began a new system of crop rotation on his farms to restore its fertility. He also tried out new machinery, including a threshing machine that was built by a millwright at Monticello in 1796 and was based on a model imported from England.

16+
THE AGE OF WOMEN
who labored beside men in "gangs" of enslaved field workers.

JEFFERSON'S PLOW
To improve performance of his plows, Jefferson redesigned the moldboard—the wooden part that lifts and turns the sod—using the principle of the wedge as the "instrument of least resistance." This plow was built by Robert L. Self in 1986.

✳ THE PEOPLE

George Granger, Sr.

While Jefferson was in Paris, he directed that George Granger, Sr. (1730–1799) tend his orchards and vineyards. In 1796, Jefferson made Granger, whom he called "Great George," the only African-American overseer at Monticello, and gave him an annual wage. Put in charge of 50 farm laborers, Granger evidently struggled with his role as both a slave and a manager of slaves. Although the first tobacco crop raised under his supervision failed, the second was praised by Jefferson as "extraordinary." Granger, his wife, Ursula, and their son, George, died within months of each other in 1799 and 1800, victims of illness treated by a folk healer.

THIS 1868 ENGRAVING, ENTITLED "STACKING HAY," DEPICTS AFRICAN-AMERICAN FIELD-WORKERS IN RURAL VIRGINIA.

STABLE
HEMMINGS CABIN
SLAVE DWELLING
SLAVE DWELLING
TEXTILE WORKSHOP
SLAVE DWELLING
SLAVE DWELLING
SLAVE DWELLING
"STOREHOUS FOR IRON"

Life on Mulberry Row

NAMED FOR THE MULBERRY TREES planted along it, Mulberry Row was the dynamic, industrial hub of Jefferson's 5,000-acre enterprise. The 1,300-foot-long section of the road that paralleled the Monticello house was the center of work and domestic life for dozens of enslaved people, free blacks, and free and indentured white workmen. To make the plantation more self-sufficient during difficult economic times, Jefferson added light industries here to build his house and support daily life. Changing over time as structures were built, removed, or repurposed, Mulberry Row had more than 25 workshops, dwellings, and storage buildings for weavers, spinners, blacksmiths, tinsmiths, nailmakers, carpenters, sawyers, charcoal burners, stablemen, joiners, or domestic servants.

PEARLWARE TEA SAUCER FROM THE SMOKEHOUSE/DAIRY

STOREHOUSE FOR IRON

Built around 1793, this 16-foot-by-10.5-foot log structure was recently reconstructed based on archaeological and documentary evidence. Jefferson referred to it as a "storehouse for nailrod & other iron," but it also was a site for tinsmithing, nailmaking, and domestic life. Isaac Granger Jefferson recalled that he "carried on the tin-business two years—it failed."

> *"Every article is made on his farm: his negroes are cabinet makers, carpenters, masons, bricklayers, smiths, &c."* —Duc de La Rochefoucauld-Liancourt

"JOINER'S SHOP"

LEFT BEHIND
Unearthed artifacts, like the nail rod below, reflect the functions of the shops on Mulberry Row, such as the blacksmith, carpenter shops, and the joinery.

THE RAW MATERIAL FOR NAILS WAS CALLED "NAIL ROD."

25+
STRUCTURES,
including dwellings, workshops, and sheds, lined Mulberry Row.

✳ THE TIMES

John Hemmings
The youngest son of Betty Hemmings, John was a skillful woodworker who eventually became head joiner on Mulberry Row, where he and his wife lived in a slave cabin. Hemmings used hand planes, chisels, saws, lathes, and other specialized tools to shape and then join pieces of pine, cherry, or other wood that had been dried in the carpenter's shop to fashion furniture, doors, balusters, sashes, and other items for Monticello. Hemmings likely made several Campeachy chairs, also known as "siesta chairs," which Jefferson was very fond of. During a bout of rheumatism while at Poplar Forest, Jefferson specifically requested one from Monticello: "I longed for a Siesta chair . . . send by Henry the one made by Johnny Hemings . . ." When Hemmings worked at Poplar Forest, he regularly wrote detailed letters to Jefferson to report on progress and discuss construction problems. He was one of five slaves freed in Jefferson's will.

CAMPEACHY CHAIRS HAVE RECLINING BACKS AND CURULE BASES.

Archaeology at Monticello

New Views of Plantation Slavery

AIDED BY JEFFERSON'S HABIT of keeping extensive records, historical and archaeological research at Monticello has made it the best studied plantation in the United States. Archaeological evidence since the 1950s has revealed new details about the plantation's landscape and architecture, as well as about the lives of enslaved people who lived along Mulberry Row. Ceramics found on the site, for example, signal that slaves were active consumers in the local economy, able to earn money and buy household goods.

"NEGRO QUARTER"
CIRCA 1770S TO CIRCA 1790

"BUILDING O"
CIRCA 1770S TO CIRCA 1801

"BUILDING S"
CIRCA 1793 TO CIRCA 1830

UNDERSTANDING LIFE ON THE PLANTATION

Every year archaeological research on the plantation landscape leads to the discovery of sites that were once the homes of enslaved agricultural laborers. Archaeologists are learning how and why their houses, yards, diets, and possessions differed from those of the enslaved artisans and domestics who lived and worked on Mulberry Row.

FRAGMENTS FROM A WILD ROSE PEARLWARE PLATE (CIRCA 1795 TO CIRCA 1820) FOUND IN THE SLAVE DWELLING "BUILDING S"

r, which as well as s. and t. are servants houses of wood, with wooden chimnies, and earth floors . . ." —Thomas Jefferson

Excavations have also provided information on nine slave dwellings across the plantation. Documentary and archaeological evidence suggests that until the 1790s, slaves at Monticello lived in barracks-style, multifamily housing. Beginning in the early 1790s, Jefferson built single-family houses for enslaved people. Abundant artifacts discovered at these sites by archaeologists reveal much about the lives of these families. ❖

FOUND OBJECTS

Discovered at Mulberry Row, items like the jaw harp, clay marbles, and a pocket-knife are clues to how precious leisure time was spent. A slate pencil and copper upholstery tack (below) found during excavation of the joiner's shop reflect the skilled work done here.

BONE DOMINOES: FROM "BUILDING S"

MOUTH HARP: FROM "BUILDING N"

FOLDING KNIFE: FROM "BUILDING L"

MARBLES: FROM AROUND THE MOUNTAINTOP

750,000

ARTIFACTS

were excavated on Mulberry Row.

HEMMINGS CABIN

Woodworker John Hemmings and his wife, Priscilla, likely lived in a cabin like this reconstruction. It represents one of three built circa 1793 on Mulberry Row for individual families. When re-creating this cabin, builders used traditional materials and methods. It is furnished based on historical records and a rare first-person account.

The Revolutionary Garden

EVER A MAN OF THE ENLIGHTENMENT, Jefferson in 1812 divided his vegetable garden into 24 rational plots, or "squares," according to the part of the plant to be harvested: fruits (tomatoes, beans), roots (beets), and leaves (lettuce, cabbage). Built on a terrace facing southeast with a 1,000-foot-long retaining wall, the garden was a grand experiment. "I am curious to select only one or two of the *best* species or variety of every garden vegetable, and to reject all others," Jefferson wrote. He kept meticulous notes on the day seeds were sowed or plants harvested. To supply salads, Jefferson had lettuce and radishes planted every week. Elderly slaves did most of the gardening, directed by enslaved head gardeners.

MONTICELLO'S GARDENERS USED TERRA-COTTA POTS TO BLANCH SEA KALE.

PEA-GROWING CONTEST

Jefferson loved English peas, planting as many as 15 types a year. He and his neighbors competed each spring to see who could bring the first peas to the table. The winner held a community dinner that included a dish with peas.

20 BEAN VARIETIES

were grown, from lima beans to scarlet runners.

NOVEL SPECIES

Of the 330 fruit, vegetable, and herb varieties grown at Monticello, many were new to American gardens, including tomatoes, rutabagas, artichokes, eggplants, broccoli, cauliflower, lima beans, peanuts, and cabbage-like sea kale.

no occupation is so delightful to me as the culture of the earth, & no culture comparable to that of the garden." —Thomas Jefferson

Ornamental Farm

JEFFERSON AIMED TO GIVE Monticello the qualities of an ornamental farm by "interspersing the articles of husbandry with the attributes of a garden." Combining utility with beauty, for example, he interspersed rows of purple, white, and green sprouting broccoli in the vegetable garden, and planted cherry trees along the garden's flank to provide shade and color. On the mountain's northwestern slope, Jefferson designated 18 acres of woods as a grove, where undergrowth was to be removed and trees thinned and pruned in the style of an ornamental forest. One visitor to Monticello remarked on Jefferson's fondness for his "pet trees."

CARACALLA BEAN
(VIGNA CARACALLA)

✳ THE TIMES

Thomas Jefferson Center for Historic Plants

During his decades of research, Jefferson corresponded with leading botanists and nurserymen, collecting and distributing plants and seeds from many parts of the world. Today, the Thomas Jefferson Center for Historic Plants at Monticello performs a similar mission, collecting, preserving, and distributing plants known in early American gardens. Although the Center's main focus is on the plants Jefferson grew at Monticello and his other horticultural interests, the program also covers the broad history of plants cultivated in America through the 19th century. Visitors to Monticello may purchase historic plants and seeds as well as books and reproduction flowerpots at the Garden Shop in the Visitor Center or online.

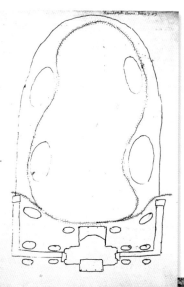

TWINLEAF
(*JEFFERSONIA DIPHYLLA*)

WINDING WALK

In 1808 Jefferson wrote to his granddaughter Ann Cary Randolph that "I have resumed an idea . . . of a winding walk . . . with a narrow border of flowers on each side." In 1812, the border was divided into ten-foot sections, each with a different flower, including *Jeffersonia diphylla* (above), a perennial of the Barberry family named after the Founding Father.

JEFFERSON'S 1807 SKETCH WITH ITS CURVING WALK REFLECTS HIS INTEREST IN AN INFORMAL STYLE OF LANDSCAPE DESIGN.

The Fruitery

OF ALL THE FRUITS in Monticello's six-acre South Orchard, peaches were Jefferson's favorite. He planted as many as 38 varieties, and wrote to his daughter Martha in 1815: "we abound in the luxury of the peach." Most peaches were used to make brandy, but some, like the Heath Cling, were raised for the table. Together with the North Orchard, where cider apples were grown; "berry squares," where currants, gooseberries, raspberries, and figs were cultivated; a nursery; and two small vineyards, where Jefferson experimented with wine grapes, the complex comprised what Jefferson in 1814 called "the Fruitery."

FIG
Jefferson brought cuttings of figs to Monticello from France.

APPLE
Among Jefferson's favorites was the Newtown Pippin, a dessert apple.

CHERRY
Jefferson grew at least 14 varieties of cherries.

"When he walked in the garden and would call the children to go with him, we raced after and before him. . . He would gather fruit for us, seek out the ripest figs, or bring down the cherries from on high above our heads . . ." —Virginia Jefferson Trist

FRUIT TREES

Jefferson's earliest plantings included olives, almonds, pomegranates, and figs. Later he raised trees better suited to Virginia's climate, such as cherries, apricots, pears, plums, and nectarines.

PEAR

An American variety Jefferson planted, the Seckel, was noted for its spicy flavor and hardiness.

24

GRAPE VARIETIES

from Europe were planted at Monticello in 1807.

1 WEST LAWN, WHERE A FLOWER BORDER BLOOMS IN SEASON

2 GARDEN PAVILION MIDWAY ALONG THE RETAINING WALL

3 BERRY SQUARES FOR CURRANTS, GOOSE-BERRIES, AND RASPBERRIES

4 SOUTH ORCHARD WITH APPLE, PEACH, CHERRY, AND OTHER TREES

5 SOUTHWEST VINEYARD SITED BELOW THE GARDEN WALL

6 WEST END OF THE VEGETABLE GARDEN

7 SUBMURAL BEDS, WHERE FIGS WERE GROWN

THE VINEYARDS

Though he enjoyed French wines at his dinner table, Jefferson never produced drinkable wines with European grapes (*Vitis vinifera*) from Monticello's vineyards, despite decades of attempts. His most ambitious try was in 1807, when he planted 24 European varieties. He also experimented with North American varieties such as the fox grape (*V. labrusca*) and the southern muscadine (*V. rotundifolia*), known as Scuppernong.

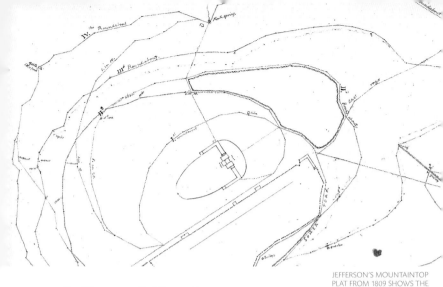

Jefferson's Roads

TO CONNECT THE VARIOUS gardens, orchards, workshops, and quarter farms on his plantation, Jefferson built a network of roads that followed the natural contours of the surrounding landscape. A series of loops, which he called roundabouts, were arranged in concentric circles at four different elevations, from lower on the mountain to the top, and were connected by diagonal roads. Named for their proportional rise in elevation, the "1 in 10 Road" was twice as steep as the "1 in 20 Road." During his frequent inspections of the plantation, Jefferson commonly traveled up to ten miles a day, on foot and horseback, without leaving his property, which stretched four miles end to end.

0.526

MILE

The circumference of the First Roundabout. Jefferson, who learned surveying from his father, recorded it in 1778. He updated the measurement in 1806 to 0.529 mile.

WINDING ROADS

Although visitors could approach Monticello from three directions via four roads, every traveler's journey ended by twisting and turning to the top of the mountain along the four roundabouts and their diagonal connector roads.

Thomas Jefferson's Grave

A PATH FROM THE SOUTHWEST end of Mulberry Row leads to Thomas Jefferson's final resting place in a family cemetery still owned by descendants of his daughters Martha and Maria. This was the location, according to family tradition, of a large oak tree under which Jefferson and his childhood friend Dabney Carr often studied. They made a pact that when one died, the other would bury him under the tree. In 1773, at age 30, Jefferson kept his promise, burying Carr in the first grave of the cemetery. On July 4, 1826, the 50th anniversary of the adoption of the Declaration of Independence, Jefferson died at Monticello and was buried the next day in the family graveyard.

OBELISK TOMBSTONE

Near the end of his life, Jefferson wrote a letter with instructions for his gravestone. He described the materials it should be built with—"coarse stone . . . that no one might be tempted hereafter to destroy it for the value of the materials"—and he wrote his own epitaph, specifying "the following inscription, & not a word more."

Here was buried
Thomas Jefferson
Author of the
Declaration of
American Independence
of the Statute of Virginia
for religious freedom
& Father of the
University of Virginia

1883

THE NEW MONUMENT WAS ERECTED.
The original obelisk, chipped by visitors, was moved to the University of Missouri.

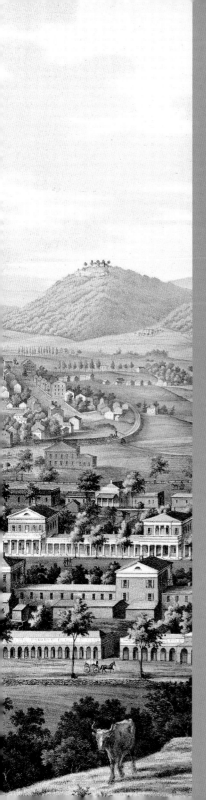

The Neighborhood

Jefferson founded the University
of Virginia just west of the town
of Charlottesville in 1819.

Jefferson's Neighborhood and Beyond

ENTRAL VIRGINIA WAS an impressive neighborhood in the early 1800s, with Jefferson at Monticello; James Madison, who succeeded Jefferson as president, at Montpelier in Orange; and James Monroe, the nation's fifth president, at Highland, just three miles from Monticello. Both Madison and Monroe were close friends of Jefferson, who sought to create a "rational society" in the Charlottesville area for the enjoyment of "philosophical" evenings "life is of no value but as it brings gratifications," he wrote to Madison "among the most valuable of these is rational society. it informs the mind, sweetens the temper, chears our spirits, and promotes health." As part of his campaign to establish a public university in Charlottesvil Jefferson not only secured funding for the school, but he also designe the campus, planned the curriculum, and recruited the faculty. Monroe and Madison served on the school's first Board of Visitors.

"*no other sure foundation can be devised for the preservation of freedom, and happiness [than the diffusion of knowledge among the people].*" —Thomas Jefferson

The University of Virginia, which opened on March 7, 1825, is shown in this hand-colored engraving after a drawing by William Goodacre, 1831.

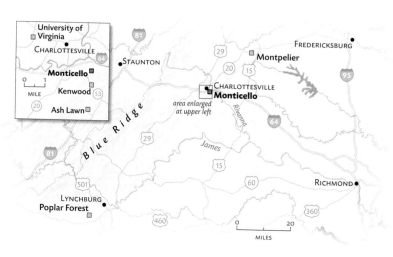

" *Wherever the people are well informed they can be trusted with their own government.* " —**Thomas Jefferson**

University of Virginia

THE FARMLAND NEAR Charlottesville that Jefferson selected in 1817 for a public university is today the heart of a leading center of research and education. Still referred to as "Mr. Jefferson's University," the institution comprises 11 schools—including arts and sciences, business, engineering, law, medicine, and public policy—with 21,000 students who proudly call themselves "Wahoos." Known for their honor code and service-oriented secret societies, students are designated as first year, second year, third year, and fourth year (rather than freshmen, sophomores, juniors, and seniors), in keeping with Jefferson's belief that learning is a lifelong process. In 1987 the "academical village" and Monticello were designated as a UNESCO World Heritage site for Jefferson's architectural design and embodiment of his ideas.

✳ THE TIMES

The Rotunda

Jefferson designed the Rotunda, modeled after the Pantheon in Rome, to serve as the new university's library. In keeping with his beliefs of the Enlightenment, he wanted the school's most prominent structure to be a symbol of reason and learning, rather than a chapel, as was typical of campuses at the time. Like his house at Monticello, the Rotunda was built with a dramatic dome room with a glass oculus in the ceiling. Following the construction of Alderman Library in 1937, the Rotunda has been used mainly for lectures, meetings, and dinners. Restoration has largely reinstated Jefferson's design.

PERHAPS THE BEST KNOWN SYMBOL OF THE UNIVERSITY, THE ROTUNDA STANDS AT THE NORTH END OF THE LAWN.

1895

FIRE GUTTED THE ROTUNDA.
It was rebuilt with a larger dome room, designed by architect Stanford White.

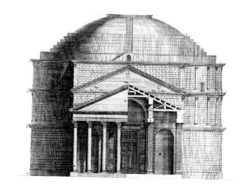

THE ROTUNDA WAS HALF AS HIGH AND WIDE AS THE ROMAN PANTHEON. PALLADIO'S DRAWING OF THE PANTHEON, ABOVE, INSPIRED JEFFERSON.

Mr. Jefferson's University

The Founder's Vision

"**I** HAVE LONG HAD UNDER contemplation . . . an university in Virginia which should comprehend all the sciences useful to us, & none others," Jefferson wrote in 1814. Consistent with the beliefs he expressed in the Virginia Statute for Religious Freedom, Jefferson envisioned a nonsectarian institution "so broad & liberal & *modern*, as to be worth patronising with the public support." As well as teaching medicine and law, it would

54

FOURTH-YEAR STUDENTS

are selected each year to live in Lawn rooms.

ACADEMICAL VILLAGE

Following Jefferson's design, two rows of five pavilions flank the Lawn south of the Rotunda. Each originally had classrooms on the lower floors and housing for a professor and his family above. Today faculty still occupy the pavilions. Connecting them are one-room dormitory residences for some fourth-year students. Behind the pavilions are private yards and gardens. Two outer "Ranges" have six "Hotels," originally dining halls, now office space, connected by housing for some graduate students.

SERPENTINE WALLS

Curved walls separate garde behind pavilions on the Law Jefferson was said to have admired the practicality of the design, which allows wa to be only a single brick thic In East Anglia, northwest of London, where such walls ar also found, they're known as crinkle-crankle walls.

this institution will be based on the illimitable freedom of the human mind . . ." —Thomas Jefferson

train leaders in practical affairs and public service. The ideal setting for such a university would be an "academical village" surrounding a broad, terraced lawn, where students and faculty would live, eat, and study together. "A plain small house for the school and lodging of each professor is best," he wrote. "These connected by covered ways out of which the rooms of students should open . . ." ❋

1 ROTUNDA: COMPLETED IN 1826; RESTORED 2014-16

2 EAST AND WEST RANGES: SINGLE-ROOM HOUSING FOR GRADUATE STUDENTS, WITH FIREPLACES

3 PAVILIONS: EACH INSPIRED BY A CLASSICAL BUILDING

4 HOTELS: FORMERLY DINING HALLS, NOW USED FOR OFFICES AND EVENTS

5 LAWN ROOMS: PRESTIGIOUS UNDERGRADUATE DORMITORIES WITH FIREPLACES, FACING THE LAWN

6 PAVILION GARDENS: RESTORED AND MAINTAINED BY THE GARDEN CLUB OF VIRGINIA

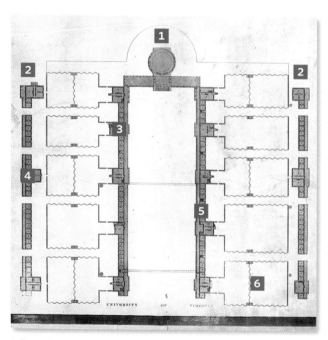

Jefferson's 1822 plan of the University of Virginia, engraved by Peter Maverick after a drawing by John Neilson.

Poplar Forest

IN 1806 JEFFERSON LAID the foundation for a second home at Poplar Forest, a working plantation his wife had inherited near Lynchburg, a three-day carriage ride from Monticello. He designed the house to be an octagon, with several octagonal rooms—"the best dwelling house in the state, except that of Monticello," he claimed. Following his retirement from politics in 1809, Jefferson used the house as a private retreat. "I have fixed myself comfortably, keep some books here, bring others occasionally, am in the solitude of a hermit, and quite at leisure to attend to my absent friends," he wrote in 1811. Here at Poplar Forest, his granddaughter Ellen Randolph remarked, Jefferson found "rest, leisure, power to carry on his favorite pursuits—to think, to study, to read."

✳ THE PEOPLE

Francis Eppes

When Thomas Jefferson died in 1826, Poplar Forest was willed to his grandson, Francis Eppes, who had been living there with his wife. Eppes, 24, was the only surviving child of Jefferson's daughter Maria Jefferson Eppes and her husband John Wayles Eppes. Along with the house, Eppes inherited 1,074 acres of the 4,819-acre plantation. On it, Jefferson had profitably raised tobacco and wheat for many years, using the labor of several generations of slaves, many of whom he inherited from his father-in-law. Eppes sold Poplar Forest in 1828.

2

MONTHS
was the time Jefferson and his family stayed at Poplar Forest when British occupied Monticello in 1781.

FIVE-SIDED "SQUINT" BRICKS WERE USED TO CONSTRUCT THE OCTAGONAL HOUSE.

VISITING POPLAR FOREST

Guided tours of the house are offered daily from 10 a.m. to 4 p.m. (from mid-March through December), and on winter weekends from 10 a.m. to 3 p.m. (mid-January to mid-March). Tours last about 40 minutes. In addition to the guided tour, visitors may walk the grounds guided by brochures that describe the landscape and plantation community, and see exhibits on the history and restoration of the property. The site is owned and operated by the nonprofit Corporation for Jefferson's Poplar Forest.

A "WING OF OFFICES" EXTENDING FROM THE HOUSE INCLUDED A KITCHEN, COOK'S ROOM, AND SMOKEHOUSE.

OCTAGONAL PLAN

The main level of Jefferson's house at Poplar Forest consisted of four elongated octagonal spaces surrounding a perfect cube. On the north side, an entry passage led directly into the central dining room, which had a dramatic 20-foot-high ceiling with a large skylight. Flanking the dining room were two chambers divided by alcove beds. On the south side was a parlor with floor-to-ceiling windows and doors. Jefferson kept a library at Poplar Forest of more than 1,000 books in a variety of languages.

POPLAR FOREST'S TALL DOORS AND PORTICOS MIRROR ELEMENTS OF MONTICELLO.

JEFFERSON CREATED AN ORNAMENTAL LANDSCAPE AROUND THE HOUSE.

JAMES MONROE

A fellow Virginian and Revolutionary War hero, the nation's fifth president was a protégé of Thomas Jefferson, who praised Monroe's scrupulous sense of honor, writing, "a better man cannot be."

28
MILES

from Montpelier to Monticello was a full day's journey in the early 1800s.

Highland and Montpelier

JAMES MONROE BUILT HIS "cabin castle" on land adjacent to Monticello that he purchased in 1793. Guided tours of the house are available daily at Highland (above), which is owned and operated by the College of William and Mary. Montpelier (below), the family plantation of James and Dolley Madison in Orange, Virginia, was recently restored by the Montpelier Foundation and the National Trust for Historic Preservation. Visitors are invited to take a 45-minute guided tour of the mansion or explore the 2,650 acres of gardens and grounds.

MONTPELIER

When James and Dolley Madison moved to Montpelier in 1797, they expanded the Georgian house his father had built, creating separate quarters for Madison's parents and themselves.

Robert H. Smith International Center for Jefferson Studies

FOUNDED IN 1994, the ICJS is the scholarly division of the Thomas Jefferson Foundation, the private, nonprofit organization that owns and operates Monticello. The Center's campus—located at nearby Kenwood, a 78-acre property once owned by Jefferson—includes the Jefferson Library, the Kenwood house, and the Roosevelt Cottage, where President Franklin D. Roosevelt sometimes stayed during his occasional retreats. Through a fellowship program, international conferences, workshops, and lectures, the Center maintains a network of scholars, teachers, and students who engage in a dialogue with Jefferson's ideas. The Center's departments include archaeology, research, publications, adult enrichment, and the editorial operations of *The Papers of Thomas Jefferson: Retirement Series.*

JEFFERSON LIBRARY

Serving scholars, teachers, students, and other researchers, the 15,000-square-foot library is a technologically sophisticated facility that houses Monticello's unique research collection. The library's online catalog, the Thomas Jefferson Portal (*tjportal.worldcat.org*), offers a wide range of resources, including unpublished reports and audiovisual media.

15,000

TITLES

are in the Jefferson Library, on archaeology, plants, education, and other topics.

✻ THE PEOPLE

International Reach

The Robert H. Smith International Center for Jefferson Studies has organized dozens of academic conferences and seminars at institutions in Australia, China, Cuba, Russia, the Czech Republic, Germany, Britain, Poland, Austria, and Italy to engage a global audience in Jefferson's ideas. Among the prominent historians who have participated in these international symposia are Annette Gordon-Reed, Jon Meacham (right, at left), Gordon Wood, Peter S. Onuf, and David Armitage. The center also regularly hosts lectures, informal talks, and panel discussions with invited speakers, visiting researchers, and Monticello scholars.

Annual Events

Jefferson's Birthday and Founder's Day

APRIL 13

Monticello marks the anniversary of Thomas Jefferson's birth with a free celebration and ceremony on the West Lawn, featuring a keynote address by the recipient of the Thomas Jefferson Foundation Medal in Citizen Leadership. Each year on Jefferson's birthday, the Thomas Jefferson Foundation at Monticello and the University of Virginia jointly present their highest honors, the Thomas Jefferson Foundation Medals in architecture, law, and citizen leadership. The awards represent subject areas that Jefferson excelled in and held in high regard.

Historic Garden Week in Virginia

APRIL

MONTICELLO IN APRIL

Each spring visitors are welcomed to over 250 of Virginia's most beautiful gardens, homes, and historic landmarks during an eight-day statewide event described as "America's Largest Open House." Make Monticello a part of your Historic Garden Week visit, and enjoy peak springtime color, programs with gardening experts, and special tours of Monticello's gardens and the Thomas Jefferson Center for Historic Plants.

Monticello's Independence Day Celebration and Naturalization Ceremony welcomes visitors of all ages.

John Lewis, U.S. congressman from Georgia, received the Thomas Jefferson Foundation Medal in Citizen Leadership in 2015.

The Fourth of July

JULY 4

There is no more inspirational place to celebrate the Fourth of July than Monticello, the home of the author of the Declaration of Independence. Since 1963, more than 3,000 people from every corner of the globe have taken the oath of citizenship at the annual Monticello Independence Day Celebration and Naturalization Ceremony— the oldest continuous naturalization ceremony held outside of a courtroom in the United States. The real meaning of the Fourth of July is found in the mosaic of stories told by the nation's newest citizens as they address the crowd at Monticello. Annual festivities include remarks by a featured speaker, a Jeffersonian Open House, patriotic music, and more.

Workshops, garden tours, and more greet visitors to the annual Heritage Harvest Festival.

The Heritage Harvest Festival at Monticello

SEPTEMBER

Thomas Jefferson, noted epicure and "ardent farmer," championed plant experimentation and soil conservation. The Heritage Harvest Festival at Monticello celebrates Jefferson's legacy as a revolutionary gardener and America's "first foodie" with more than 100 educational programs; hands-on workshops; garden tours; a bounty of heirloom fruit and vegetable tastings; lessons on seed saving and gardening; an organic, local food marketplace; kids' activities; and more. Each September, this family-friendly event, cohosted by Monticello and Southern Exposure Seed Exchange, is held on the breathtaking West Lawn of Monticello.

Visiting Charlottesville

Thomas Jefferson's legacy in education, innovation, food, wine, and gardening flourishes today in his hometown. Nestled amid the foothills of the magnificent Blue Ridge Mountains and about 110 miles south of Washington, D.C., Charlottesville and Albemarle County are home to a thriving urban community, more than 700 square miles of natural beauty to explore, and the University of Virginia, one of the nation's top public universities. Named the "Best Place to Live in America" and "Locavore Capitol of the World," the area boasts a top wine region, the most eateries per capita in America, the best running trails in the United States, and more. Learn more at *visitcharlottesville.org*.

The pedestrian mall in downtown Charlottesville features some 150 shops and eateries.

Further Information and Suggested Reading

For information on planning a visit to Monticello, educational materials, and online shopping, consult the Thomas Jefferson Foundation website, *monticello.org;* the website contains extensive research sources, including the Thomas Jefferson Encyclopedia. For transcriptions of the writings of Jefferson and other founders, visit *founders.archives.gov.*

Biographical Works

The Road to Monticello: The Life and Mind of Thomas Jefferson, Kevin J. Hayes (2008)

Thomas Jefferson, Richard B. Bernstein (2003)

Thomas Jefferson: A Brief Biography, Dumas Malone (1993)

Thomas Jefferson: The Art of Power, Jon Meacham (2012)

Jefferson's Writings

Jefferson's Memorandum Books: Accounts, with Legal Records and Miscellany, 1767–1826, James A. Bear, Jr. and Lucia C. Stanton, eds. (1997)

The Papers of Thomas Jefferson, Julian P. Boyd and others, eds. (1950)

The Papers of Thomas Jefferson: Retirement Series, J. Jefferson Looney, ed. (2004)

The Words of Thomas Jefferson, Thomas Jefferson Foundation (2008)

Thomas Jefferson: Writings, Merrill D. Peterson, ed. (1984)

The Quotable Jefferson, John P. Kaminski, ed. (2006)

On Monticello

Monticello in Measured Drawings, William L. Beiswanger (2011)

Thomas Jefferson's Monticello, Thomas Jefferson Foundation (2002)

"A Rich Spot of Earth": Thomas Jefferson's Revolutionary Garden, Peter J. Hatch (2012)

Saving Monticello: The Levy Family's Epic Quest to Rescue the House that Jefferson Built, Marc Leepson (2003)

Jefferson and Monticello: The Biography of a Builder, Jack McLaughlin (1988)

The Worlds of Thomas Jefferson at Monticello, Susan R. Stein (1993)

Political Thought and Legacy

Emperor of Liberty: Thomas Jefferson's Foreign Policy, Francis D. Cogliano (2014)

To Begin the World Anew: The Genius and Ambiguities of the American Founders, Bernard Bailyn (2003)

The Mind of Thomas Jefferson, Peter S. Onuf (2007)

The Plantation and Its People

The Hemingses of Monticello: An American Family, Annette Gordon-Reed (2008)

Sally Hemings and Thomas Jefferson: History, Memory, and Civic Culture, Jan Ellen Lewis and Peter S. Onuf (1999)

"Those Who Labor for My Happiness": Slavery at Thomas Jefferson's Monticello, Lucia C. Stanton (2012)

Thomas Jefferson's Garden Book, Edwin M. Betts, ed. (1944)

Jefferson's Interests and Special Topics

Thomas Jefferson's Granddaughter in Queen Victoria's England: The Travel Diary of Ellen Wayles Coolidge, 1838–1839, Ann Lucas Birle and Lisa A. Francavilla, eds. (2011)

Jefferson's Shadow: The Story of His Science, Keith Thomson (2012)

Dining at Monticello: In Good Taste and Abundance, Damon Lee Fowler, ed. (2005)

The Jeffersons at Shadwell, Susan Kern (2010)

Monticello

After Thomas Jefferson

THE AUCTION OF JEFFERSON'S PERSONAL PROPERTY ON JANUARY 15, 1827, WAS ADVERTISED IN VIRGINIA NEWSPAPERS.

1827 Jefferson's slaves and household furnishings publically auctioned at Monticello.

1831 Monticello purchased by James T. Barclay.

1834 Monticello purchased by Uriah P. Levy.

1879 Jefferson Monroe Levy acquired Monticello from his uncle's estate.

1923 The Thomas Jefferson Memorial Foundation purchased Monticello.

1937–41 Substantial restoration and reconstruction of house and grounds undertaken.

1953–54 Structural renovations of the house undertaken and a central heating and air-conditioning system installed.

WILLIAM ROADS MADE THIS FIRST KNOWN PHOTOGRAPH OF MONTICELLO IN 1867–68.

AFTER STRUCTURAL REPAIRS IN 1954, WORKERS REINSTALLED THE PARLOR'S PARQUET FLOOR.

1957– Present Archaeological excavations of landscape features, Mulberry Row, and sites associated with free and enslaved workers are ongoing.

1978 First planting made in re-created Grove.

1981 One thousand-foot-long garden wall reconstructed.

1982 First trees planted in re-created South Orchard.

1984 Garden Pavilion reconstructed.

1987 Monticello named to World Heritage List; Center for Historic Plants established.

1991–95 Archaeological excavations undertaken at Shadwell.

APPROXIMATELY 100 DESCENDANTS OF MONTICELLO'S ENSLAVED FAMILIES GATHERED ON THE WEST PORTICO OF MONTICELLO IN 1997.

1993 Commemoration of 250th anniversary of Jefferson's birth. For the exhibition "The Worlds of Thomas Jefferson at Monticello," 150 objects were returned to Monticello. "Getting Word," an oral history project on descendants of Monticello slaves, was also launched.

1995 International Center for Jefferson Studies dedicated.

1996 Thomas Jefferson Parkway ground-breaking took place.

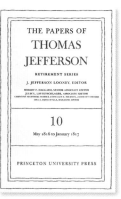

COMPILATION OF THOMAS JEFFERSON'S PAPERS

1999 *The Papers of Thomas Jefferson: Retirement Series* was launched at Monticello.

2001 The dependencies restoration was begun with the Cook's Room, followed by the Kitchen (2004) and Wine Cellar (2010).

2002 Jefferson Library, Thomas Jefferson Parkway, Kemper Park, Saunders-Monticello Trail, and Saunders Bridge dedicated

2004 Purchase of Montalto, Jefferson's "high mountain." Bicentennial of the Lewis and Clark expedition was commemorated at Monticello.

2009 Thomas Jefferson Visitor Center and Smith Education Center opened.

2011 The Robert H. Smith Center at Montalto opened after restoration of "Repose."

THE POPULAR "SLAVERY AT JEFFERSON'S MONTICELLO" EXHIBITION TRAVELED TO FOUR AMERICAN MUSEUMS.

2012 "Slavery at Jefferson's Monticello: Paradox of Liberty" exhibition opened at the Smithsonian National Museum of American History.

2015 Restoration and interpretation of Mulberry Row and Monticello's upper floors was commemorated. Visitor Center was named for David M. Rubenstein.

DAVID M. RUBENSTEIN (LEFT) AND LESLIE GREENE BOWMAN, PRESIDENT, AND DONALD A. KING, JR., CHAIRMAN, OF THE THOMAS JEFFERSON FOUNDATION AT THE DEDICATION OF THE RUBENSTEIN VISITOR CENTER

Support for the Restoration of Monticello

The Thomas Jefferson Foundation gratefully acknowledges these individuals and organizations for their leadership gifts and grants since 2010 in support of Monticello's restoration:

Mountaintop Project
David M. Rubenstein
Mr. and Mrs. John H. Birdsall
Robert H. Smith Family Foundation
W. L. Lyons Brown III
Stuart R. Brown
Cary Brown Epstein
The Joseph and Robert Cornell Memorial Foundation
The Mary Morton Parsons Foundation
Sally and Joe Gladden
The Manning Family Foundation
Jan Karon
Mr. Ronald S. Kossar
Caterpillar
The Beirne Carter Foundation
Tommy and Kemp Hill

Cabinet
Grady and Lori Durham and Family

Bed Chamber
David and Susan Goode and Family

Library
Christopher J. Toomey

Martha Jefferson Randolph's Room
Ms. Charlotte Moss and Mr. Barry Friedberg

Dining Room
Polo Ralph Lauren

Mulberry Row
Fritz and Claudine Kundrun
National Endowment for the Humanities
Richard S. Reynolds Foundation
The Mars Family
The Cabell Foundation
Mr. and Mrs. Richard A. Mayo

Stable
The Sarah and Ross Perot, Jr. Foundation

Kitchen Road
Garden Club of Virginia

Robert L. Self, Monticello's former Robert H. Smith Director of Restoration, planes a reconstructed finial while restoring the North Privy.

Index

Page numbers in **bold**
indicate illustrations.

Illustrations Credits

All photos courtesy Thomas Jefferson Foundation (TJF), including images by Jack Looney, Edward Owen, Robert Llewellyn, The Griffin Discovery Room, Keith Damiani, Robert Lautman, Harlow Chandler, Leah Stearns, Mathias Tornqvist, Gail McIntosh, Philip Beaurline, Cameron Davidson, Bill Moretz, Floyd Johnson, Carol Highsmith, Eleanor Gould, Mia Magruder, Walter S. Smalling, Caitlin Hepner, and Shaking Hands Productions, except as otherwise noted.

Cover (CTR), Courtesy of Independence National Historical Park; Back Cover (UP RT), Isaac (Granger) Jefferson by unknown photographer, 1845. Tracy W. McGregor Library of American History. Special Collections, University of Virginia Library; Back Cover (LO), Gift of the Gilder Lehrman Collection; Spine, Courtesy of Independence National Historical Park; Front Flap, Library of Congress, Manuscript Division; 1, Ivan Schwartz with StudioEIS; 5 (CTR), Rare Book Division, New York Public Library, Astor, Lenox, and Tilden Foundations; 5 (LO), Karen Blaha/ 21ma. com/wiki.php?title=File:Serpentine_wall_UVa_daffodils_2010. jpg/creativecommons.org/licenses/by-sa/2.0/deed.en; 11, Ivan Schwartz with StudioEIS; 12 (UP), Martha Wayles Jefferson Bell. Courtesy of The Moorland-Spingarn Research Center, Manuscript Division, Howard University, Washington, D.C.; 12 (LO), Library of Congress, Manuscript Division; 14 (UP), Jefferson's Portable Desk, Courtesy of the Division of Political History, The National Museum of American History, Smithsonian Institution; 14 (CTR), Declaration of Independence, oil on canvas, painted by John Trumbull, ca 1818. Architect of the Capitol; 14 (LO LE), National Portrait Gallery, Smithsonian Institution; gift of an anonymous donor, NPG.75.414; 14 (LO CTR LE), The Colonial Williamsburg Foundation, Virginia; 14 (LO RT), The White House Historical Association (White House Collection); 15, Library of Congress, Manuscript Division; 17 (LO), Courtesy of Independence National Historical Park; 19 (UP), Hans A. Rosbach/no.wikipedia.org/wiki/Villa_Cornaro#/ media/File:VillaCornaro_2007_07_14_front_1.jpg/http://cre-ativecommons.org/licenses/by-sa/3.0/legalcode; 19 (LO), Front Elevation of the Rotunda (N328). The Thomas Jefferson Papers, Albert and Shirley Small Special Collections, University of Virginia Library; 20-21, Monticello: 1st version (elevation), probably before March 1771, by Thomas Jefferson (N48; K23). Courtesy of the Massachusetts Historical Society; 22 (UP), Image courtesy Missouri Botanical Garden, www.botanicus.org; 23 (UP), Gift of the Gilder Lehrman Collection; 24 (UP), Library of Congress, Prints and Photographs Division, HABS, "HABS VA, 2-CHAR. V,1- (sheet 16 of 32)"; 25 (UP), Portrait of Uriah Levy, Courtesy of U.S. Naval Academy Museum; 25 (LO), Monticello, West Front, ca 1870. Special Collections, University of Virginia; 34 (UP), TJF, made by John Isaac Hawkins, ca 1806; 35 (UP LE), USA, Inc. (www.BuildWithUSA.com); 40-41 (LO), Library of Congress, Prints and Photographs Division, HABS, "HABS VA, 2-CHAR. V,1- (sheet 20 of 32)"; 41 (UP), Courtesy of Independence National Historical Park; 46 (LO LE), Public Domain; 66 (UP LE), Courtesy National Portrait Gallery, Smithsonian Institution, and TJF; 71 (CTR RT), Monticello: portico and terrace benches, 1 sheet, 2 pages, after 1801, by Thomas Jefferson (N147ff; K147ff). Courtesy of the Massachusetts Historical Society; 75 (CTR), TJF, Jefferson's Walking Stick courtesy of James Madison's Montpelier Collection; 75 (LO), Portrait of Mrs. James Madison (1768–1849), painted by Bass Otis. Collection of The New-York Historical Society; 77 (UP RT), Monticello: main stairs, Probably 1771, by Thomas Jefferson (N51; K26). Courtesy of the Massachusetts Historical Society; 85 (LO), Monticello: curve of dome, [1796], by Thomas Jefferson (N147d; K149d). Courtesy of the Massachusetts Historical Society; 91 (UP RT), Garden Book, 1766–1824, page 45, by Thomas Jefferson. Courtesy of the Massachusetts Historical Society; 95 (UP RT), Library of Congress, Manuscript Division; 96 (LO), Wendell P. Dabney, Cincinnati's Colored Citizens (Cincinnati, 1926); 97 (CTR), public domain; 98 (UP RT), Library of Congress, Manuscript Division; 103, Maryland Historical Society; 104 (UP), Isaac (Granger) Jefferson by unknown photographer, 1845. Tracy W. McGregor Library of American History, Special Collections, University of Virginia Library; 104 (LO), September 14, 1769 issue of the Virginia Gazette. Courtesy of the Virginia Historical Society; 105 (LO), Farm Book, 1774–1824, page 24, by Thomas Jefferson. Courtesy of the Massachusetts Historical Society; 106 (UP), Farm Book, 1774–1824, page 18, by Thomas Jefferson. Courtesy of the Massachusetts Historical Society; 106 (LO), Courtesy of Special Collections, University of Virginia Library; 107 (LO LE), Portrait of Colonel John Wayles Jefferson. Courtesy of the Museum of Wisconsin Art; 108 (UP), The Mill at Shadwell. Special Collections, University of Virginia Library; 109 (UP), Monticello: re: crop rotation, undated, by Thomas Jefferson (N230; K169e). Courtesy of the Massachusetts Historical Society; 109 (LO), Library of Congress, Morgan collection of Civil War drawings; 110-11 (UP), © 2017 Thomas Jefferson Foundation, created by RenderSphere Inc.; 117 (LE), Monticello: letter and garden/flow-erbeds (layout), verso, 7 June 1807, by Thomas Jefferson (N147gg; M15). Courtesy of the Massachusetts Historical Society; 117 (RT), Wikimedia Commons, Kevin Gepford; 119 (UP RT), Rare Book Division, New York Public Library, Astor, Lenox, and Tilden Foundations; 120 (UP), Monticello: mountaintop (plat), 1809, by Thomas Jefferson (N225; K169). Courtesy of the Massachusetts Historical Society; 121 (RT), Library of Congress, Manuscript Division; 122-3, View of the University of Virginia, Charlottesville and Monticello, taken from Lewis Mountain. Albert and Shirley Small Special Collections, University of Virginia Library; 124-5, Academic Village Engraving by W. Goodacre, ca 1831. Special Collections, University of Virginia Library; 126, Groganvision, Dan Grogan; 127 (UP), Wikimedia Commons, Aaron Josephson; 128 (CTR), Flickr Creative Commons, Karen Blaha; 128-9, View of the Lawn at the University of Virginia, Courtesy of Garth Anderson; 129, Architectural Map of the UVa Campus Academic Village. The Thomas Jefferson Papers, Albert and Shirley Small Special Collections, University of Virginia Library; 130 (UP), State Archives of Florida, Florida Memory, http://floridamemory.com/items/show/26290; 130 (CTR), Courtesy The Corporation for Jefferson's Poplar Forest; 130-131 (LO), Courtesy The Corporation for Jefferson's Poplar Forest; 131 (UP), Courtesy The Corporation for Jefferson's Poplar Forest; 131 (CTR), Cross Section of Poplar Forest (N350). The Thomas Jefferson Papers, Albert and Shirley Small Special Collections, University of Virginia Library; 131 (LO LE), Courtesy The Corporation for Jefferson's Poplar Forest; 131 (LO RT), Courtesy The Corporation for Jefferson's Poplar Forest; 132 (UP), Photo by Jared Ladia Photography, Courtesy Ash-Lawn Highland; 132 (CTR), The White House Historical Association (White House Collection); 132 (LO), Courtesy of The Montpelier Foundation; 136 (LO), Courtesy Downtown Business Association of Charlottesville; 138 (UP), Library of Congress, Manuscript Division; 138 (CTR), Monticello, East Front, ca 1834. Special Collections, University of Virginia; 139 (UP RT), View of "Slavery at Jefferson's Monticello: Paradox of Liberty" exhibition at the Smithsonian, Courtesy of The National Museum of African American History and Culture, Smithsonian Institution.

**Monticello: The Official Guide
to Thomas Jefferson's World**
Charley Miller and Peter Miller

Published by the National Geographic Society
Gary E. Knell, *President and Chief Executive Officer*
John M. Fahey, *Chairman of the Board*
Declan Moore, *Chief Media Officer*
Chris Johns, *Chief Content Officer*

Prepared by the Book Division
Hector Sierra, *Senior Vice President and General Manager*
Lisa Thomas, *Senior Vice President and Editorial Director*
Jonathan Halling, *Creative Director*
Marianne R. Koszorus, *Design Director*
Barbara A. Noe, *Senior Editor*
R. Gary Colbert, *Production Director*
Jennifer A. Thornton, *Director of Managing Editorial*
Susan S. Blair, *Director of Photography*
Meredith C. Wilcox, *Director, Administration
and Rights Clearance*

Staff for This Book
Barbara Brownell Grogan, *Editor and Text Editor*
Marty Ittner, *Art Director*
Charles Kogod, *Illustrations Editor*
Carl Mehler, *Director of Maps*
Terra Carta, *Map Production*
Marshall Kiker, *Associate Managing Editor*
Judith Klein, *Senior Production Editor*
Rock Wheeler, *Rights Clearance Specialist*
Katie Olsen, *Design Production Specialist*
Nicole Miller, *Design Production Assistant*
Bobby Barr, *Manager, Production Services*

Thomas Jefferson Foundation
Leslie Greene Bowman, *President*
Ann H. Taylor, *Executive Vice President*
Susan R. Stein, *Richard Gilder Senior Curator
and Vice President for Museum Programs*
Gary Sandling, *Vice President of Visitor
Programs and Services*
Fraser Neiman, *Director of Archaeology*
Gabriele Rausse, *Director of Gardens & Grounds*
Gardiner Hallock, *Interim Director of Restoration*
Joshua Scott, *Director of Development*
Sharon McElroy, *Director of Retail Sales*
J. Jefferson Looney, *Editor, Papers of
Thomas Jefferson Retirement Series*
Lisa Francavilla, *Managing Editor, Papers
of Thomas Jefferson Retirement Series*
Paula Viterbo, *Editorial Assistant, Papers
of Thomas Jefferson Retirement Series*
Derek Wheeler, *Research Archaeologist*
Emilie Johnson, *Assistant Curator*
Diane Ehrenpreis, *Assistant Curator*
Peggy Cornett, *Curator of Plants*
Eleanor Gould, *Curator of Gardens*
Mia Magruder, *Marketing Assistant*
Madeleine Rhondeau, *Digital Services Coordinator*
Keith Damiani, *Project Manager*

National Geographic Partners
1145 17th Street NW
Washington, DC 20036-4688 USA

Get closer to National Geographic explorers and photographers, and connect with our global community. Join us today at nationalgeographic.com/join

For information about special discounts for bulk purchases, please contact National Geographic Books Special Sales:
specialsales@natgeo.com

For rights or permissions inquiries, please contact National Geographic Books Subsidiary Rights:
bookrights@natgeo.com

**Library of Congress
Cataloging-in-Publication Data**
Miller, Charley, author.
  Monticello : the official guide to Thomas Jefferson's world / Peter Miller and Charley Miller ; introduction by Leslie Greene Bowman.
    pages cm
  Includes index.
  ISBN 978-1-4262-1506-3 (hardcover : alk. paper) --
ISBN 978-1-4262-1507-0 (pbk. : alk. paper)
  1. Monticello (Va.)--Guidebooks. 2. Jefferson, Thomas, 1743-1826--Homes and haunts--Virginia. I. Miller, Peter, 1949- author. II. Title.
  E332.74.M54 2016
  975.5'482--dc23

                                        2015028710

Printed in China

18/PPS/3